Tyra -
Have a happy
Birthday - I enjoy
and appreciate your
friendship -
Love
Tricia

The
Power
in Being a
Woman

Anita Canfield

ISBN: 0–934126–62–3

3rd Printing

May 1987

Randall Book Company
1182 N. Industrial Park Drive
Orem, UT 84057

Printed in the United States of America

Contents

Chapter  One

The Power Within You

IMAGINE WITH me the different desires for power that we see all around us.

Somewhere in a far away town a weak and frightened woman *struggles for power* as she tries to tread a domineering, unsympathetic husband's drowning wave to control her.

In an exclusive suburb, in a palatial mansion with a driveway lined in evergreens, another woman *seeks power* in her appearance to the world as she picks up the phone and dials an exclusive shoppe to order several thousand dollars worth of apparel.

In a smaller neighborhood nearby where rows of houses are all the same, an apathetic, uninterested woman *whines for power* as she succumbs to arguing the insolvable with her teenage children.

I see a church down the road where a confused and threatened woman *searches for power*, as—observing well-ordered lives around her—she frantically takes on more work than she can handle to prove to herself she is as good as everyone else seems.

There is a platform in a distant city being prepared for an aggressive and convinced woman who is determined to *hold onto power* as she presses her political views forward to a waiting public.

In an office on a busy workday is an energetic and dedicated woman who tries to *juggle power* as she manages career, home, and family.

In a hospital bed lies a very young and eager woman cradling a new baby in her arms and trying very hard to *understand new power* in her life. Even in this same hospital is another woman in another bed who has *exercised power* over her own body and has had an abortion.

And at the side of her bed somewhere today, still another woman kneels and begs to *know the power* of God, if there be any.

I want *power* in my life! How about you? I don't want any of the Three D's in my life: discrimination, disillusionment, and depression. I want to become everything a woman can possibly, humanly, divinely become, and so do you!

We've been friends long enough that I can confide in you that I have sought power from virtually every *external* source I could in my life. And not until I discovered that *true power* comes only from within (and not without) did I begin to feel that kind of control in my life that conquers discrimination, disillusionment, and depression.

Certainly external sources bring us some powers. We are going to discuss those as "parts to the whole" in this book. They are important, but they do not produce the real inner power that causes our lives to change.

The real power within each of us doesn't come from our accomplishments, our credits, our talents, our skills, our husbands, our children, our houses, or clothes, or possessions. It doesn't come from our church callings or church status, nor does it come from our education, our goals, our careers, our clubs, our community work, or the kind of car we drive.

The *real power within each of us* has been given to us to enable us to accomplish, gain, and hold to far more than we ever dreamed possible for ourselves. The real power within each of us is the *power* to become like God. It is *His* power, and the way this power comes into being in our own lives is through the Holy Ghost.

A woman who wrote to me shared the struggle for power in her life and described it as a battle within herself. Part of her letter captured the simple and great principle of the only true power within us:

... A few years ago I faced a trial in my life that sent me into depression. ... Although I am a person who seeks the light of Christ and have had a strong testimony, I didn't think I could conquer this situation. The battle *within* was fierce. Satan was so deceiving in very small ways. After a year of tears one afternoon, the *spirit spoke to me*, and *I finally listened.*

It was then I realized I cannot change what I face, but I can be strong and live the gospel of love. My spirit self had had enough tears and self-pity; my soul hungered for happiness. The Savior was near. I reached for his hand. I recorded in my journal: "I am becoming a true daughter of God. There is *tremendous power within* to be the very best, to see the best in others, and to live the best we can!

I loved her insight! She didn't say there is a tremendous *desire* or *drive* within to be the best, etc. No, she said it perfectly: There is a tremendous *power within* each of us to so succeed.

My sister Renee was throwing away old magazines and papers she had accumulated over the years when she came across the issue of *Life Magazine* that published the first pictures of the human fetus. There in beautiful color was the first photograph of a living human embryo only a few weeks old, photographed through a special microscope as it was absolutely invisible to the naked eye.

As Renee stared at it and lingered over its reality and miracle, she couldn't help but once again marvel that even in its microscopic form it possessed *everything* necessary to be an adult human being. Contained within that embryo was every organ, tissue, bone, and marrow that would develop into an adult body. That microscopic embryo was unrecognizable as a human adult, and yet that's exactly what it was to become.

An intelligent being in the image of God possesses every organ, attribute, sense, sympathy, affection that is possessed by God himself. ... But these are possessed by man, in his rudimentary state, ... or in other words, these attributes are in *embryo*; and are to be gradually developed (Parley P. Pratt, *Key to Theology*, pp. 100-01).

3

This single illustration that the Lord has given to us as a rememberance of our real purpose in life is more exciting to me than any other concept! Through the human embryo developing *intact* into an adult we see the great shadow of what is to come. We do not go through life from infancy "finding parts of ourselves" that will make us adults, like longer legs, bigger stomachs, larger ears. We already have them; they simply develop.

As the fetus is the adult body in embryo, so we are the God in spiritual embryo. We will not go through life "finding parts of a God" that will make us gods, like charity, mercy, patience, humility. We already have them; they already exist *within* each of us. As we unlayer our weaknesses, we allow more room for them to develop. The key to this development and unlayering is the Holy Ghost.

In each of us already exist the qualities that God the Father and God the Mother possess. Just as we inherit eye color, noses, dimples from our mortal parents, so have we inherited the "organs, attributes, senses, sympathies, and affections" that our heavenly parents possess. Just as our mortal parents feed us, clothe us, clean us, and shelter us so that our infant bodies have every chance possible to mature into adults, our heavenly parents also spiritually feed us, clothe us in blessings, clean us through repentance, and shelter us with their love. They do this through the gift and power of the Holy Ghost.

Since we cannot be in our heavenly parents' presence at this time, the Holy Ghost has agreed to remain a personage of spirit so he can dwell with each of us. He adapts himself spiritually somehow to these inherited senses, sympathies, attributes, etc. and *refines them.* He does this to the degree *we* allow him to teach, inspire, and comfort us.

The ordinance of confirmation says, "Receive the Holy Ghost." This word *receive* suggests some action on our part, that we need to reach out and receive him into our lives. There is a price to be paid to become fluent in the language of the spirit in order to identify feelings and senses, to experience change, and eventually power. If we are willing to expend the effort, we will have the *reality* of a great teacher and comforter near us! "Draw near unto me, and I will draw near unto you" (D&C 88:63).

Living righteously is the primary step to receiving the spirit, but it's only the first step. It is important that we strive to be spiritually minded as well. We know that we cannot be spiritually minded unless we are righteous, but can we be righteous and not be spiritually minded?

Remember your beginning algebra? Let's do some deductive reasoning. Remember the formula:

$$\text{If } A = B$$
$$\text{and } B = C$$
$$\text{then } A = C$$

One day reading in 2 Nephi 9:39 I discovered what being spiritually minded means. It said, ". . . to be spiritually minded is life eternal." Remembering another often quoted scripture in John 17:3, "and this is life eternal to know thee, the only true God and Jesus Christ whom thou has sent," I then deduced that to be spiritually minded is to know the only true God and Jesus Christ whom he sent.

So the answer to the question can we be righteous and not be spiritually mind is *yes*. We can be externally doing what is right—going to church, active, obeying the word of wisdom, etc. and yet, not know God.

We get to know God by drawing near unto him through the Holy Ghost. This is a *tremendous power within* each of us to do this. It is accomplished by applying the following principles:

We Must Have Faith

We have to have faith in God and that what he intends for us is good and for our own good, faith in who we are (daughters of God) and what we can become (Goddesses). "And Christ hath said: If ye will have faith in me, ye shall have *power*. . ." (Mormon 7:33; emphasis added).

If we lose our faith, we lose the true perspective of perfection. We become overwhelmed with the idea that perfection is an arriving instead of a striving. If we lose faith in God and in ourselves, we begin to believe that unless our behavior is perfect we are worthless.

Perfection is *not* what is important in mortality, but rather what is important is the *consistency in striving for perfection!* Then perfection becomes the *result*, the *process* of the behavior, and not the behavior itself. Perfect behavior, even when we brush against it, is pretty hard to perform one hundred percent of the time. But being consistent in striving for perfection is something we can accomplish every day.

The Lord tells us—commands us—to be as perfect as his Father which is in Heaven because if he set the goal lower than that, we'd never really reach it. Unless our reach exceeds our grasp we can never be sure of all we can attain.

Studying the scriptures can increase our knowledge of God, and as we study we will have more faith in him and live closer to the Holy Ghost.

Several years ago we were having a dinner party, and shortly before the guests arrived, I discovered I had forgotten to buy the whipping cream for the dessert. We lived three miles from the nearest store and several more miles from other ones. Steve gladly offered to get me some and hurry back in time for company to arrive. He was gone until the last minute and came in breathless. "I went to two stores, and they were out of whipping cream. The lady in the last one showed me all the different substitutes. She showed me the frozen kind, the kind in a can, and the powder you mix up. Anita, I hope I did the right thing. I just stood there and pretended I was you and made a choice."

From the paper bag he pulled the frozen kind, *exactly* what I would have picked. How did he know that? Because he knew *me*. He tried to think as I would think. To know God is to know what he thinks, and that can be done by reading the scriptures.

Recently I shared this advice with a beautiful woman who said simply, "Okay, I'll try it." Several weeks later she said, "It is so simple. I've heard that counsel all of my life. I never had faith in it until now. I wish I could stand on the rooftop and shout to everyone, 'It really works!' Reading the scriptures every day *does* make a big difference."

If it didn't make any difference, I don't believe the Lord would ask us to do it. Knowing his mind—getting to know him through his own words—truly increases our faith. As we do that, we are more open and dependent on the Holy Ghost.

Last year one of my large design jobs in Southern California was a beautiful home overlooking the ocean. After one year planning and ordering, the installation was now ready. We traveled there with a crew of nine people and two semi trucks full of furniture, accessories, even dishes and linens.

The clients had left for four days to allow us the time and freedom to install the entire house. They were returning at noon on Saturday and were expecting guests from Texas later that day.

With that scale of a project it took eight hours just to unpack the trucks. Then we began to sort and move and place furniture and decor. We feverishly worked late into the nights, putting in twenty-one hour days. Just compacting the trash occupied one person's time. Friday night came, and I finally sent everyone to bed at 2:00 a.m. Then I walked from room to room surveying what needed to be done to meet the 12:00 noon deadline. It would take exact chores from each member if we were to make it. I wrote lists for everyone describing what they needed to do. Then I went to bed. Suddenly I realized there was not an alarm clock in the entire house. It was now 3:00 a.m. I knew I had to be up at 6:00 in order to awaken everyone. If we didn't get up at 6:00, we'd never make the noon deadline.

There wasn't anything to do but ask for help. I had no other choice but to have faith. Faith needed to be a *power* for me that moment. I simply told our Father that there wasn't an alarm clock, and I needed to be awakened at 6:00 a.m. sharp. I explained how hard we'd worked, how much energy, time, and money were riding on this job. I told him that we'd given it everything but simply had forgotten a clock. Would he help awaken me at 6:00 a.m.? Then I crashed into a deep sleep.

It seemed only moments had passed, and suddenly I heard a voice. "It's 6:00 a.m." Opening my eyes, I saw faint morning light and the fog. Then I looked at my watch. It was 6:00 a.m. *exactly*. I know who had said it. It was the Holy Ghost. My faith grew stronger in that experience, and indeed it was *power*. It gave me the feeling that we had the power to succeed. This feeling had nothing to do with talent, money, circumstance, or any other external source. The feeling of power came from an internal source, *a power within*.

Understand The Adversary

Satan was given the power to bruise our heels, or in other words, to render us incapable of progress or accomplishment if we choose to let him. But the greater power given to us—the power to crush his head—guarantees us we can succeed and be victorious over him. It is our charge to understand he is continually working against the kingdom, which really means he is working against us. "All things which are good cometh of God. And that which is evil cometh of the devil" (Mormon 7:12).

In Scotland a group of ministers angrily confronted the mission president with the question, "What right do the Mormons have in Scotland?"

The mission president calmly said that as he understood it, there were two powers or influences in the world. The one that represented goodness, brotherly kindness, love, and fairness came from God. Did they agree? Of course, they did. Then he said he understood that bitterness, envy, hatred, pride came from Satan. Did they agree with that, too? They did. Then he asked, "If any of you have any of those feelings in your hearts toward me or my church, where did you get them?"

Embarrassed and apologetic, they realized the source of their resentment.

Analyze your own thoughts by asking, "Do these thoughts leave me uplifted, inspired, motivated, determined to be a better woman?" Or do your thoughts leave you spiritually and emotionally poor and weak?

A good sister in one of the wards in Zion was called to be the cub scout leader in her ward. Having never done anything like this before, she was very nervous, yet accepted eagerly the challenge to do a good job. Partly because of her personality (she was blunt and energetic) and partly because of her inexperience, she offended some of the parents. When she discovered her mistake, she tried to make amends by personally visiting each one with a loving and sincere apology. Individually, they felt compassion for her and all seemed well in control until these parents got together.

As they rehashed her weaknesses, they began to rekindle their anger and to judge, judging all areas of her life. They went to the bishop and demanded her release. He called all of them together, including this sister, to discuss and—hopefully—resolve the situation. The couples became even more hostile and began to criticize her ability as a mother. When no solution looked eminent and the bishop could see that the "discussion" was getting out of hand, he rebuked the couples and dismissed them.

This good woman was devastated. Though she had tried to do right, she had made mistakes. No matter what the bishop said, she could not be comforted as she returned home. As the days passed, she continued to be bombarded by the memory of their stinging, cutting words. She resolved not to go back to church again. Then slowly, but ever so surely, the Holy Ghost began to heal her broken heart. He reminded her that this was not their church; it was the Savior's church. He made her realize that the weak thoughts of worthlessness she had embraced were not from God but from Satan. He reassured her that she could learn to forgive. But the real *power within* came to her as she realized that counsel and comfort from the Holy Ghost was uplifting and inspiring. For the first time in her life she could see that despair had not come from God.

The "D's" have nothing to do with God. Discrimination, disillusionment, despair, depression, doubt, discouragement all begin with the first letter of Satan's name, Devil.

A very close friend of mine was called into the office of one of the high councilors of her stake. He had called her in, he said, to interview her for a stake position. He remarked that he had "heard" that she was an opinionated woman with an abrasive personality. He told her that she had given a mini class at stake leadership the month before because he wanted to "check her out" before extending the call. He informed her that he had hidden a tape recorder in the room that evening and taped her entire class. Then he proceeded to tell her what he liked and disliked about her. He made it clear she was not his choice for the position but that the stake organization wanted her.

It was all she could do to contain her tears. She held them in until she got home. She phoned me immediately and broke down and sobbed and sobbed. "Why, Anita? I wouldn't do that to him."

Do you think she felt defeated or inspired at his "counsel"? As she was able to recognize where those feelings and words came from, she was able to be healed and comforted by the Holy Ghost. The adversary will defeat us; the Lord will inspire us—even with the *same* words! It's the *feelings* they bring that tell us the truth of the source!

For example, Satan can whisper to you. "You can't change the past," and the feelings that accompany his spirit are dark and depressing. The Holy Ghost can teach us that "We can't change the past, but there is no looking back. *Press on with today!*" and the feelings that accompany his spirit fill us with deep gratitude that the Lord loves us so much. Though they are almost the same words, there is a different spirit.

Realize That Spirituality Is A Way Of Life And Not An Experience

We must learn to listen to the Holy Ghost and remain *teachable*. We should earnestly *seek* the spirit. Seeking the spirit starts with asking for it daily in our lives. The Lord is happy with us when we ask for such gifts. After asking, we should stretch our minds by pondering the gospel constantly. To those who do this the Lord has said, "I will tell you in your minds and in your heart by the Holy Ghost, which shall come upon you and which shall dwell in your heart" (D&C 8:2-3).

Joseph Smith taught that the Holy Ghost would "whisper peace and joy to [our] souls, take malice, hatred, strife, and evil in all form from [our] hearts and leave [us] with the desire to do right and to labor to bring forth the Kingdom of God" (*Conference Reports*, April 1974).

In other words, *power within us.*

The weakness that stands in our path to spirituality is pride. Pride is the great sin of the spirit. It was Lucifer's sin. Pride renders us unteachable and hardens our hearts to spirituality. "Give *ear*, be not *proud*" (Jeremiah 13:15) implies we cannot hear the spirit if we are proud.

Have you noticed the way the Lord and the prophets describe pride in the scriptures? They call it being "hard hearted." In the

Nevada desert we have *cliche* (pronounced *clee-chee*). Underneath a few inches to a few feet of loose soil are patches, even acres, of cliche. It is hard packed dirt, so hard it has to be blasted or pounded out. Not even a pick axe will budge it; it is like concrete. Therefore, when it rains, the water cannot soak into the soil but runs off the top and causes terrible flash flooding.

So it is with hard hearts. When a heart becomes hardened with pride, the spirit cannot sink into it, and we become "past feeling" (1 Nephi 17:45).

Swallowing our pride and becoming humble and teachable is not without pain.

> Correction, when it comes, often has a cutting edge and normally there is no anesthetic. Hearts which are so set upon wrong or worldly ways must first be broken, and this cannot be done without pain. . . . If some pride needs to be peeled off, off it comes, but in a time and manner our Tutor thinks best. We will feel that pain, shame, and dismay. But if we can trust Him who is doing the sculpturing of our soul . . . we have developed some of that submissiveness which is so necessary in our further development (Neal Maxwell, *Even As I Am*, p. 60).

The Holy Ghost should be a "constant flow" unto us. Dramatic experiences with the Holy Ghost for most of us are few and far between. Yet, when we discuss his presence, it seems the dramatic incidents are always mentioned, giving the impression he only visits during emergency or crisis. The Holy Ghost is and should be our way of life. Slowly I am learning how little credit he gets all day long.

Why do you think he cares about the day-to-day trivia of our living? If most of us had to depend on those earth-shattering experiences, we'd never make it. We must realize that the spirit is present and that we are obliged to pay attention, give him credit, and then obey. That is all part of becoming fluent in the language of the spirit.

He cares about our day-to-day living because he wants to help us eliminate *stress* from our lives so that we can be free to hear, learn, and do more. He wants us to have true peace, inner peace, and balance in our day-to-day lives. He wants us to feel more self-reliant and capable because we have him as an advisor.

My experiences with the "constant flow" are in the everyday mundane areas of living, nothing dramatic. He's told me to move a jar of jam off the counter. Perhaps it would have been knocked over later by a child, and there would have been stress in having to clean up another mess. He has told me to do the laundry *now*. Later, something else comes up, and I realize that if I'd delayed, I couldn't have done it. I would have suffered stress when the children had no clean clothes for school. He's told me to take a child to the library, to check on a child, to write a note, to call a ward member, to take the meat out of the freezer.

Believe me, there are so many times I haven't listened, thinking to myself, "silly thought." Then later I discover *why* I should have obeyed. In moments like these we know the difference between *power* and *power-less!*

Each of us must become friends with the Holy Ghost and depend on personal revelation if we are to unlock the real power within us. Of those who constantly suspend their own judgment to lean upon others, who supposedly have greater wisdom, Brigham Young said: "They will never be capable of entering into the Celestial Glory."

If we don't have power over ourselves, we are less able to develop the righteous power to influence others.

> . . . there are relatively few converts in the church. Many have converted in the sense that they have turned to righteousness and faith, but comparatively few declare a change in personal views. . . . Their feelings are *more accurately described* as an awakening of the *memories* of the spirit. Their so-called conversion does not consist as much in changing as it does in *identifying feelings or senses that were always theirs* (Joseph Fielding McConkie, *Seeking the Spirit*, p. 3; emphasis added).

There is a price we must pay to draw upon the real power within us. If we are willing to expend the effort, we will have a great teacher and comforter near us! This inner power will dispel *discrimination* as we feel the "constant flow" of our Father's love for us as he patiently waits out our perfecting process. In a world of abuse, the Holy Ghost not only heals, but opens our eyes to the reasons others around us are abusive.

This inner power will dispel *disillusionment* as the Holy Ghost teaches us that each person has individual gifts that not only help them, but bless lives around them. In a world plagued with disillusionment, the Holy Ghost helps us pierce the veil and see that "all these things are for our own good and experience" and help us find our full resources for the eternal world to come.

This inner power will dispel *depression*, for the Holy Ghost will not leave us comfortless. In a depressed world, the Holy Ghost lifts us out of the darkness, up and up, and up to the light and truth, even up to the keeper of the light.

The Holy Ghost will sail us across the seas of affliction. He will take us away from the deserts of spiritual poverty and help us to climb the mountains of tribulation. He will lift us out of the dark clouds of confusion and guide us safely through the valley of despair.

The Holy Ghost is the only true power within each of us. And it is real power.

> . . . be anxiously engaged in a good cause, and do *many things* of [your] own free will, and bring to pass much righteousness; for, the *power is in [you]* (D&C 58:27-8).

Chapter Two

The Power in Being Unique

THE IDEA of being unique almost seems a paradox. We want to be recognized for making a worthy contribution in our lives; we want to be viewed as "special," and yet we seem to cling so desperately to the idea that we do not want to be different from everyone else. We want to be just like everyone else so that we can feel like we belong.

We tell ourselves: "Okay, I must be a *success* because then I will have the best of both sides of the paradox. If I am a success, it will mean I'm making a worthy contribution, yet I am accepted as the successful people are."

Though that concept sounds very good, we still don't have a good definition of success! If two women came forward to define success—one of them wealthy, one very poor—we probably wouldn't believe either one. If the wealthy woman said that success has nothing to do with money or fame, we would laugh and say that she could say that because she *has it.* If the woman of no material means said money and fame has nothing to do with success, we would laugh and say that of course she says so, as she doesn't have it!

We usually accept as our personal standard of success those set by our parents, friends, and society. We live our whole lives trying to keep up with those standards. We actually believe that we are born into life like blank sheets of paper, and until we write on those pages our accomplishments, talents, and successes, we are worthless. We believe that we continue to be blank sheets of paper.

Our parents began fostering this quality within us, and too many of us urge these values on our own children. We say, "Honey, why don't you learn to play the piano? You'll make me so happy if you do it. If you can play the piano, I'll be so proud."

Right away this registers to us that we aren't pleasing if we don't accomplish. It implies we aren't complete or worth as much as those who accomplish, when accomplishments are just embellishments. We are already worth more than blank sheets of paper, or the Lord came to earth in vain. We are worth a great deal just because we are the daughters of God. Wouldn't it increase self-esteem to encourage these other accomplishments in a more positive tone, such as: "Why don't you try playing the piano? It may be a wonderful resource for you and a talent you may not know about."

Most of us are going to miss out on the world's biggest successes: the Pulitzer, the Nobel, the Oscar, Tony, and Emmy. Only a handful of us will have fame in the world; a few more of us will be known across the nation; and maybe if we live our whole lives in one place, we'll be recognized in our community. The majority of us will come to earth and go to our graves personally and spiritually intimate with less than one hundred people.

How can the majority of us then really know success? Can we truly be unique, different, and yet be a part of the group? Can we "belong" and not be overwhelmed by the uniqueness of others? Can we be a part of something so massive (like the Mormon Woman Image) and yet retain uniqueness and individuality?

Recently I read something that Elder Maxwell wrote that not only opened my eyes to the answers to those questions but also electrified me. He wrote:

> So it is that in studying and writing about Jesus, one realizes that in the Savior we are confronted with a real personality . . . *a genuine and real personality*. This latter dimension of his divinity is often subordinated, however unintentionally, to his roles and missions (Neal A. Maxwell, *Even As I Am*, p. 32; emphasis added).

It suddenly made me realize that Jesus has a *personality* separated from his *qualities*. It inspired me to realize that we can become like Jesus, rather we *are* to become like him *with* our *personalities*. Adapting his *qualities* such as charity, meekness, humility, patience, etc., has nothing to do with our *personalities*. We will become like the godhead and yet retain our individuality and personality just as they have done! Of course, as we refine these qualities, our personalities will also develop into perfection. Can you imagine multitudes of personalities influencing each other without fear, rejection, or jealousy?

We are to become like them, exercising our free agency, not as a mass unit but individually. Each of us is so exquisitely different; no two lives ever parallel each other. Certainly we share many of the same trials, tests, experiences, but the way we look at them and learn from them is as unique as is each person.

> God's refusal to overwhelm and to conform mankind by his sheer power reflects not only his gentleness but also his justice. He desires to preserve our free agency ... [and I might add also our uniqueness]. The Father and our Savior desire to lead us through love, for if we were merely driven where they wish us to go, we would not be worthy to be there, and surely we could not stay there. They are shepherds, not sheepherders. If, however, we freely follow—coming, experience upon experience, to be more like them, ... then will come the resplendent reunion and the *unending and ultimate belonging* (Neal A. Maxwell, *Even As I Am*, p. 21; emphasis added).

It seems we struggle most for self-esteem in the *area* of being unique. Self-esteem is more important to us than anything. Without it we feel "power-less."

When our self-esteem is so heavily dependent on other's opinions of whether or not we are a success, we are not free to make our own choices. Or if we are trapped in that pit of comparing ourselves to those around us (the Mormon Mold Image), we are not free to make intelligent decisions based on our goals, talents, and personalities. We then, indeed, become power*less* to know real success. We are truly not free to be unique!

Being Unique Is Important

The first important step in feeling the power in being unique must come from *gaining a testimony that to be unique is important.* "For all have not every gift given unto them, for there are many gifts, and to every man is given a gift by the Spirit of God" (D&C 46:11).

The Lord said it: to *every* man and woman is given a gift, at least one gift. And I believe him.

But this knowledge isn't going to do you any good unless you believe it, unless you ask him to confirm it. We have to communicate with our Father in Heaven in order to understand him and feel his love. It is really as simple as asking him. "Is this true; do I have a gift?"

The parable of the ten talents helped me to gain a testimony of the importance of our gifts and that we each have at least one. Read that story over often and read those verses in the scriptures that have to do with "gifts." Spending time with the perfect words of perfect men brings us closer to them and closer to the testimonies we seek.

There is a story Melvin J. Ballard related about Orson F. Whitney that illustrates what being a success really means.

> The last time I visited my dear friend, Orson F. Whitney, he was in great distress, and I knew it was my last visit with him. I was bidding him goodbye, and I knew the end was at hand. He told me that he thought he had brought on this illness through overwork; that instead of resting through a little vacation period he had devoted himself to writing the story of his life. He said, "I am not going to leave my family any stocks, bonds, any mortgages, or money in the bank. All I have is my little home. The only thing I will leave them is the story of my life. . . . I had not written the story and so I devoted myself to prepare the story. . . . I finished it, and last Christmas I gave my children and my grandchildren the story of my life (Melvin J. Ballard, *Through Memory's Halls*).

It is the story of his sacrifices, the story of the price he paid, and the struggle he went through to subscribe to the gospel of Jesus Christ and to become a servant of the Master, *to develop the gifts and talents that were in him.* "There is only one thing I am leaving in this world that is worth anything," he said. "It is my family. If some day they, too, can come where I am, I will be rich. I will have everything that life offers that is worth anything."

Do you think Elder Whitney felt successful? Elder Orson F. Whitney was a great man in the Church. He performed much service for his God and Savior. He not only served the Saints. He loved them. He accomplished this through his *uniqueness.*

We are all the Lord has to work with. He can't get the work done without us. He works *through* our personalities to accomplish his work. He works with us also *according* to our personalities.

Again, Elder Maxwell's thoughts on the apostles' mission:

> While the fundamental and summational content of the testimony of all the special witnesses in behalf of the Savior will be the same, the manner in which the witness is given and the emphasis within that witness will, of necessity, *differ with the personalities of these men* (Neal A. Maxwell, *Even As I Am*, p. 10; emphasis added).

We must each gain a testimony of the value of our uniqueness and personality and cherish that knowledge.

Steve Morris tells the story of how a woman he met understood the importance of being unique and helped him shape his life.

Steve, born in Saginaw, Michigan, was blind. In his elementary school years, he moved to a house on Hastings Street in Detroit. It was here in this city that he met a woman who gave him the courage to be unique, a woman who understood the power in being unique. It was his grade school teacher, Mrs. Beneducci.

She was a very wise woman and realized that mere words of encouragement or inspiration didn't carry much weight to a blind nine-year-old boy. But the day came when she was able to teach him a life-long lesson on uniqueness.

One morning she walked into the classroom of noisy, rowdy children. As Mrs. Beneducci began the class, she stopped and listened to a noise she heard. "What was that? I heard a noise! It sounds like scratching? My goodness, I think it's a mouse!"

The girls screamed, the boys cheered. A few climbed on desks. "Oh, calm down now," Mrs. Beneducci said. "Steve, will you help me find the mouse?"

Steve brightened, sat up straight in his chair and said eagerly, "Okay, now everybody be really quiet." Then he leaned his head down, turned it in another direction, and then pinpointed the wastebasket. The mouse was discovered!—discovered by Steve Morris who had a remarkable pair of ears developed in compensation for having been denied eyes since birth.

The class finally settled down. The mouse was caught and removed from the room but not from the heart of small, unseeing Steve. A pride was born within him and is with him still.

Mrs. Beneducci continued to encourage and support and inspire Steve as he began to develop his uniqueness into a great talent. The marvelous ears of Steve Morris gave popular music a singer-composer, a musician, the producer of five Grammys, thirty gold singles, and eight platinum records. Steve Morris—from the time he was nine years old in Mrs. Beneducci's class—was never known as anything but "Little Stevie Wonder."

Seek Uniqueness

"Seek ye earnestly the best gifts" (D&C 46:8).

Go after the best gifts, the ones you innately know are yours! Ask for them, *seek* them! Where can we start to look for them, the gifts we *came* with?

First, look in your patriarchal blessings. Since I first shared the idea about "dissecting" our patriarchal blessings, numerous sisters have told me that for them it was a turning point. The idea is so simple, but the results are profound. Take a piece of paper and list four headings:

COUNSEL   WARNINGS   GIFTS   PROMISES

Then, line by line through your blessing, place the words under one of those headings. A personality will look back across the page at you. You will see a woman who has *always* existed. The same woman that Father knows. You are better able to see the gifts *you came here with*!

The second place to look is in our church callings. By accepting them, even if we feel we can't do it, we are opening a door to discovery. The Lord *will not* open any doors for us. He'll bring us to them, but we have to do the opening! Many great women in the church have become so because of their callings in the Church. Dwan Young, the General President of the Primary, has said many times she has developed in her capability because of her service among the children in Primary.

> The Lord does not begin by asking about our ability, but only about our availability. And when we prove our dependability, He will increase our capability (Neal A. Maxwell).

Third, pay attention to those familiar feelings within you. Pay attention to the compliments you hear. The familiar feelings about specific tasks or tools in your life are *innate* (things you came with) gifts and memories.

Fourth, become educated. Women think that with education they may need to make the choices to either seek fulfillment outside the home or to sacrifice an education in order to rear a family. Or they may feel they will need to be "superwoman" and juggle career and family.

Education is so much broader and so much more personal than that! It is not a single external experience but an internal process of life! It is not to be a load on our backs to be sacrificed in the name of motherhood. But it is to be a *total awareness of our uniqueness for all our lives.*

Education is a refinement, a replenishment, an expansion of our intelligence. It is a combination of both learning and teaching. Learning and teaching exists on any and every level, whether in a classroom, your kitchen, through a professor, or a tape in your recorder. It can happen with a friend, the scriptures, a child, or in conversation with the Lord. To be an educated woman doesn't have anything to do with a formal course of instruction but everything to do with pursuing our uniqueness.

Elaine Shaw Sorenson shared the story of a member of the Church in Columbia who educated herself, sought her gifts. Hermana Cabrera has found power in her uniqueness. She lives in a tiny two-room shack, with no heat, no electricity, no plumbing. Water is brought from the plaza from a pump shared with six other families. Though Hermana Cabrera lives alone with her young children on the barest existence and has had a life filled with hardship and great trials with a formal education only long enough that she learned to read, she is educated in her uniqueness. All around her are tokens of refinement: a hand crocheted tablecloth on a rough wooden table, pictures of flowers and loved ones on the wall. Her children are refined and well mannered. She asks deep, searching, sensitive questions about the gospel. She is educating herself in a manner that is positive, mind-expanding, and unique.

A woman's influence can be limitless. Some women will choose formal, traditional routes of education and will contribute to discoveries in science, medicine, industry, and business that will change a part of society; others will write books, or create art that will challenge souls for generations. But some will make just as significant impact on humanity by their educated influence on their own sons and daughters at their own hearths. Mothers who educate themselves in the best way they know by their wonder, interest, and exhilaration are mothers such as Jochebed, who nurtured young Moses; Elizabeth who taught John; Mary who tutored Jesus; Lucy Mack Smith who reared Joseph Smith. Our challenge is to realize that our influence on our peers, families, and our posterity for generations can be limitless" (Elaine Shaw Sorenson, *Ye Are Free To Choose*).

Realize WHY We Are Unique

"To some is given one (gift) and to some is given another *that all may be profited thereby*" (D&C 45:12).

"That *all* may be profited thereby" means our gifts benefit everyone, even ourselves. We are unique so that we can be both learners and teachers, and thus have the opportunity for the fullest growth possible. If we were all lawyers, who would fix the plumbing? If we were all educators, who would sit in class? If we were all bakers, who would give us fruits and vegetables? If we were all mothers, who would help us carry the load? If we all had the same needs at the same time, who would comfort us?

> A friend doesn't ask
> Can I help with your load?
> But has already carried it
> Far up the road.

—Mary Dawson Hughes

How is this done? Is it done through our differences, through our uniqueness?

There is a woman I know about who is one of millions in the world who seem to be unique only in a negative way. She had brain damage in her infancy that has left her mentally handicapped. Life has been tough, even cruel at times for this sister of ours.

Other than her handicap, she doesn't seem so unique; in fact, she even appears rather insignificant. She's never had her name in the newspaper; she's never had public recognition; she's never made a notable contribution in her community. She will probably always remain obscure and insignificant in the eyes of the world.

She lives alone in a little, more-than-modest house. She holds down an even more modest job, wiping off tables in a restaurant. It is a job designed for the mentally handicapped. She pays her taxes; she takes care of her little house and even has a garden. She is a perfect example of what the world calls unimportant, unsuccessful, insignificant.

But, she has found success, and she is living proof that there is power in being unique because "*every* man is given a gift . . . *that all may be profited thereby*" (D&C 46:11-12).

She has a calendar in her home that has recorded in it the birthdays of every single person she knows. Not one of these special days goes uncelebrated. She mails cards or hand delivers them with flowers from her garden. Sometimes she brings a little handmade postcard. For many of her handicapped friends it's the only recognition they ever have. One elderly man who lived alone except for his cat, seemed forgotten by his family. Every Thanksgiving she walked to his house with a T.V. dinner and a can of cat food for his cat.

Her life is merely little unimportant acts of service and love. Is she unimportant? Is she unsuccessful? Not to the lives she touches. She'll never be a famous person, but she *feels* the power in being unique. She doesn't moan about the "lack ofs" in her life; she doesn't hide away her gifts because she's afraid of being ill-praised or underpaid. She doesn't lack for self-esteem because she wonders if she fits in. She simply uses her gifts "that all may be profited thereby" (including herself). She doesn't worry about being successful; she just worries about being useful.

Be Yourself

It is a decision. Don't even think about being somebody else! You are unique; you are good; you have unlimited potential! Don't be different. Just decide to be better.

The 1984 Olympics was an example in which uniqueness became power. Every one of those athletes had developed their physical uniqueness into physical *and* mental power. It was evident as personal glimpses of their individual lives were highlighted, that they had discovered early in life that they could mold their own lives. They had forsaken the norm of peer group pressures to explore their own interests and ambitions.

In sharp contrast to that was a special segment one evening on the "nightlife" after the Olympics. The commentator took the television audience from one nightclub to another showing the current social trends among young people the same ages as the Olympians. The Mods were a group who listened to music of the '50s, wore thrift store clothes, and drove Vespas. The Punk Rockers wore leather, chains, pink and purple hair, and listened to the hard rock musicians. The Stoners smoked dope, dressed like hoodlums, and drove "souped up" cars and spoke rough language. The New Wave were more trendy in dress, and they also had their own language and music and drove certain vehicles. The G.Q. were highly fashionable and wore expensive clothes, drove expensive cars, and spoke "totally" correct English. The commentator noted as he went from Mod nightclub to GQ nightclub, "It seems as if when you wear a certain style, talk a certain slang, drive a particular car, and listen to specific music, suddenly you have an identity."

What a sharp difference between watching (all day long) young people who had an identity "of their own" and then that evening seeing that same age group struggling to have an identity by being "part of the group"! We can never truly know the unlimited power within us if we don't practice being ourselves.

Let me share with you some thoughts by Mary F. Sturlaugson, a Black native of Chattanooga, Tennessee, the fifteenth of twenty-four children. She was the first person in her family to graduate from high school; she attended Dakota Wesleyan University where she graduated in English, and she is currently pursuing a master's degree in psychology. But most important, she is one who has made a choice to be herself:

> As people have become acquainted with me, there has always seemed to be a common question. I have usually not been confronted with it, but the thoughts have been there. I realized that this was often due to people's feelings of delicacy, or their inability to frame the question correctly. Usually I was approached in a half hesitant sort of way, or with eyes of curiosity, or with looks of pity and compassion. But thanks to an honest little fourth grader at Hillcrest Elementary School, the unspoken question was finally posed: "How does it feel to be black?"
>
> This morning I would like to express to you my feelings on how it feels to be black, a female, and a member of The Church of Jesus Christ of Latter-day Saints. The color of my skin has brought me great persecution, as well as the most difficult struggle in my life—the struggle of trying to help people understand that

this color is God-given, as is any other color. It is not one that was forced on me, but one that I chose to receive.

We often talk and preach about free agency in the premortal existence and in this life. But somehow we seem to fail to comprehend all that it means. Or we comprehend it to a point that is pleasing to us or convenient. Understanding what needed to be accomplished to help each of us return to our Father in Heaven, our brother Jesus Christ said, "Father, send me." Exercising our free agency, each of us also said, "Father, send me." This color—one that has definitely brought about more than its share of persecution and suffering—is the one I chose. Thanks to the beautiful principles of the gospel that were taught to me, I am now able to bear the trials I face because of my color—not with bitterness, but with a heart full of sorrow for those who do not have the understanding of these principles in their lives.

I am sure our Heavenly Father felt great joy and pride as he made the many different colors of flowers, trees, and the other things that beautify this earth. He must have felt even greater pride and joy as he placed his children of all colors upon this earth, but at times we fail to enjoy the beauty of being his children because of differences in skin color. I witness this often as people confront me and ask me what they should call me: "Black," "Negro," "Afro-American," "Colored," or what. When in doubt, I tell them, simply call me "Sister." Please do not let the color of my skin keep from you the knowledge of our eternal bond.

Being a female has also brought its share of struggles, and they have been compounded by virtue of my being black. Being a black female seems to bring with it a reputation for having low morals and similar problems, and I am still amazed at how insensitive people can be to the fact that I have feelings and specific goals in mind. Often I meet people who have seen a black man—perhaps down in Moab or some other place—and they seem to automatically feel—no matter what the guy is like—that he and I should get together, simply because of our skin color. Yet we are all taught—black and white—that we should have specific qualities in mind as we look for our eternal mate.

Being a Mormon has given me the greatest comfort I have known as I have faced my trials of being black and female. For to know the will of God is the greatest knowledge, to suffer the will of God is the greatest heroism, to do the will of God is the greatest achievement, and to have the Lord's approval of your work brings the greatest happiness (Brigham Young University, *Ye Are Free To Choose*, p. 80).

Being useful and being ourselves truly helps us to *cherish our differences* and open our eyes to our particular uniqueness as it applies to our particular missions in life. This awareness frees us from ourselves. It frees us from worrying about whether or not we "fit" or "belong" or are a "success."

Albert Einstein once wrote: "The true value of a human being is determined primarily by the measure of the sense by which he has attained *liberation from self.*"

The world tells us that to be unique means to "do your *own* thing, to look out for number one." The Lord tells us that being unique means using our talents to look out for number two, number three, number four and so on.

What is success? It is taking our uniqueness and using it to bless the world and lives around us.

What is uniqueness? Uniqueness is Sandy Jolley. Her uniqueness is *dedication.* An attractive, well-groomed young mother with five small children, she is active in pro-family groups and vigorously supports political candidates who support good moral and ethical platforms.

Against a man running in another district who was liberal, extreme leftist, and almost amoral, she single-handedly worked night and day for weeks to organize defeat. Her strong campaigning against him worked, and the opposing candidate won.

Sandy was my visiting teacher for several years. She never missed a month, even during her pregnancies. She always came prepared to stay and visit with a new gospel concept or question to jog my thinking. She also saw to it that the ward members were informed on the current district candidates, and more than once she personally visited each of us, asking us to write a letter to our congressman. Living the gospel to Sandy meant deciding to defend it, too, and her unique gift of dedication inspired many.

Uniqueness is Valerie Christiansen, who has a special gift of *cheerfulness*. When her husband was our bishop for five years, she faithfully supported him, never letting her own frustrations get in the way. I saw our bishop spend long hours in behalf of not only the ward members but anyone who needed him for a comforting hand. There must have been many times she needed him, many family plans put aside, many nights when he came home too late, many moments cancelled because he needed to be administering in his calling of bishop. Yet, not once, ever, did Valerie show her discouragement, her disappointment, or her loss. Never did she utter one word of complaint. Instead, we could *always depend* on Valerie's beautiful smile wherever she went! There was comfort in that grin from ear to ear. I loved to be around her; she always made me feel the sun was shining. Of course, Valerie didn't always feel the way she looked. But no one could really ever understand what she felt, unless, of course, they'd been a bishop's wife. But Valerie blessed the ward with her unique gift of cheerfulness.

Uniqueness is Renae Weston, whose great gift is *faith*. Renae has a darling little girl—her number four child—born with Down's Syndrome. The doctors warned her not to have another baby because the chances would be extremely high she would have another Down's baby. Renae was also subjected to other pressures not to have more children. But faith is indeed a power. Renae said to me, "If the Lord thinks I'm worthy enough to have another *perfect* spirit like Laura, I welcome it to my home. If he feels one is all I can handle, then I know this baby will be normal." She gave birth to a healthy baby girl a few months later. It really didn't matter to Renae and her husband. They would trust in God and accept his will. Renae knew the great value of spirits and especially those who are innocent. Her unique gift of faith is a great, great example to every man and woman she knows.

Uniqueness is Janet Edwards, who shared her gift of courage with us. Janet is a mother and grandmother and a very patient woman. She had a freak accident several years ago that broke her leg. She was put in a leg cast and fully expected to recover in the standard six to eight weeks time. Several weeks went by, and the doctors told her the leg wasn't healing. The weeks turned into months, and still the leg would not heal. The months turned into two long years of trial.

With each visit to the doctor she displayed more and more courage as she was repeatedly met with a "not yet." Then she faced her first operation. The doctors said it would heal faster with the painful and risky surgery. Again she was courageous as she said, "Well, let's do it." Many months later, still in another cast, came the discouraging words, a second surgery was needed. If this did not work, she would have to have the leg removed. Again, exemplary courage was all I ever saw from her. I know she suffered horrible pain and burden. Two years in a cast must be a bit of prison. But she never gave up, and she never gave in. Her unique gift of courage strengthened her family, friends, and neighbors.

Uniqueness is Denise Shipley, who has a unique gift of humility. No blowing horns or fanfare in Denise's humble attitude, but rather simple, quiet acts of service. She was the one always there taking a pie, loaf of bread, hot rolls, or dessert to someone. No new mother, new neighbor, or sick person goes unnoticed; Denise is always there. The elderly are her favorites. She makes sure they are visited and comforted and that they feel useful. I was her visiting teaching companion for almost two years. She had asked for the route nobody wanted: isolated women who lived way out of town in the desert foothills, women who were most inactive. They were women used to "roughing it," doing without a lot of city conveniences. Some of them had even refused visiting teachers, until Denise came into their lives. No fanfare, no horns blowing, she simply went about *their* business, tending to *their* wants, needs, and suffering. Her unique acts of humility never stopped, and I love her for sharing those.

Uniqueness is Carol Carlson, one of the most *honest* women I know. Carol is a great master teacher. She had prepared herself for service to the Lord by studying the gospel and then *honestly* evaluating her life in relation to the Savior's. She won't let herself get away with anything, no matter how painful it is to face. She teaches with impact because her inward honesty has helped her to clearly articulate what she has learned and is learning. She doesn't teach from a reference point of self-righteousness that squeals what vast knowledge she has. She teaches from an honest point of view, "Look, this is what I'm learning and this is *how* I'm learning it." She knows how to admit to herself, and others, her human weaknesses without apologizing for them. She faces the Lord with the same strength. No matter how much she feels like rationalizing her behavior, if negative, she just won't let herself get away with it. Her unique gift of honesty has been in itself a master teacher for many.

Uniqueness is Renee McCormick, my sister, who is a great, great *peacemaker*. What a wonderful uniqueness this is! She is truly a person without guile. She has the ability to see people's problems without seeing them in any negative light whatsoever. She then tries in a quiet way to influence them to positive approaches by making gentle references to gospel principles. She refuses to gossip or to listen to gossip.

One day she came to me and said, "Anita, I have a problem. I saw a prominent member of our ward drinking iced tea in a restaurant some time ago. For the past few weeks this person has been avoiding me, walking on the opposite side of the chapel, casting eyes away from mine, and so on. What should I do? Should I go up to that person and say that I saw the iced tea but that it doesn't matter to me? Should I tell them that it's between them and the Lord, and I love them the same and no one else knows? Or should I pretend I never saw it, go up to them and go on as nothing happened—maybe making it appear as if I didn't see it?"

Well, I looked at my sister, and in my most curious voice asked her: "Well, WHO is it?"

She replied, "Anita! I'm not going to tell you. That's gossiping."
I responded with a sly, "Oh, I'll never tell. Besides, I *need* to know so I can better answer your questions!"

Of course, I didn't need to know, and she never told me. Instead, her example and uniqueness taught me a great lesson about peacemaking.

Uniqueness is Joanne Evans who is a woman of unique perseverance. Joanne has been my secretary for nearly five years and is like part of our family. Her own large family of husband, seven children, sons and daughters-in-law and grandchildren have been blessed immeasurably by her uniqueness. They haven't had the easiest life with a family that size. Joanne has not just weathered illnesses, tragedies, trials, financial setbacks, and hostilities. She has persevered! She's the kind that doesn't "live" through life. She "works" through it with a wonderful attitude of trust in the Lord. She knows that if she does her part, everything will work out okay!

She has personally blessed my life with her uniqueness as she has attended to my many needs and put up with my many inadequacies. She has done things for me way beyond the "call of duty" as a secretary of a design firm. She has even changed diapers for me! At this time in my life the Lord sent Joanne to me so that I could be blessed by her uniqueness. She has helped me persevere when the whole world seemed against me. Her unique gift of perseverance has often been like cement, not only in my business but in my personal life as well.

Uniqueness is YOU! There are differences about you that only YOU can share and build with. Certainly other people are cheerful, courageous, peacemaking, persevering, etc. But the differences are brightened and heightened by individual *personalities*. We each have those unique gifts that become blessings to others as we use them *through* our personalities.

Our challenge is to be powerful women, powerful in our uniqueness. To first dream, then do, then learn, then teach!

> Cherish your visions, cherish your ideals, cherish the music that stirs in your heart, the beauty that forms in your mind, the loveliness that drapes your purest

thoughts. For out of all that will grow all delightful conditions, all heavenly environment. Of these, if you remain true to them, your world will at last be built!

(James Allen)

That is the potential within each of us, to be aware of all that we *are*, so that we can learn more and then teach. It is our duty to be an influence in the human condition and an influence for all eternity!

Cherish your differences. I need them in my life. My children need them. Bless my life; let me learn from you; teach my children and my posterity.

Assist me with my burdens. And, as I follow you far up the road, I become increasingly aware that the great power needed to carry the load is the power in being unique!

Chapter Three

The Power of Positive Thinking

It was October 20, 1983, in Newark, New Jersey. A group of actors called the Mercury Players had assembled together at a local radio station to dramatize H.G. Wells' novel *War of the Worlds*. As the actors and broadcasters narrated an invasion of strange warriors from the planet Mars, millions of people believed it was really happening. For hours after the broadcast there was genuine panic.

The police stations were besieged, telephones blocked, the freeways jammed. Millions of listeners believed the earth was being invaded by the Martians! My own grandmother told me it was "believable"!

How did this happen? The actors were shocked when they heard the news. They had no idea it would be taken so seriously. What was the reason?

It was because the listeners *thought* it was true! The power of thought is the strongest force in the human spirit. Our thoughts will make us or break us.

Recently I watched a television program that explored a scientific discovery that *thought* could be photographed! Through special lighting and computers the television audience saw a man silhouetted in different colors: the greater the intensity of heat in a part of the body, the warmer the color. Around his brain was the color red, indicating that it was the "warmest" or "liveliest" part of the body with the most thought. The man was given commands to hold or pick up an object or take a step forward. The moment he obeyed, the color red would appear at his feet or fingertips or wherever the body was responding.

It was absolutely fascinating to "watch" *thought*, and I began to see it clearly as, indeed, an extremely important *power!*

Thought as a power enabled Peter to walk on water. Possibly, could it be *thought* as a *power* that enables spirits or resurrected persons to travel through the veil, walk through walls, move an object? These are just ideas to suggest to you that thought truly is a *power*.

You become what you think. You are right now in a position in life that is the result of all your thinking.

What you think about begins with the power of suggestion. This is one of the important reasons we are continually counseled to stand in Holy Places: to read only good literature, to avoid "R" rated movies.

Dr. Rene Fauvel, in his book *Mein Kampf*, explained Hitler's remarkable understanding of the law of suggestion. Hitler himself spoke of the psychology of suggestion as a terrible weapon in the hands of anyone who knew how to use it. He was able to will the Germans to believe what he willed them to believe, and once that belief took hold, they started their campaign of terror. Everywhere throughout Germany appeared slogans, posters, banners, huge signs, and massed flags. Hitler's picture was everywhere. "One Reich, one Folk, one Leader" became the chant. Every group gathering sang the marching song "Today we own Germany, tomorrow the whole world." Other songs and statements such as "Germany is behind Hilter to a man," "Stand up, you are aristocrats of the Third Reich," and "Germany has waited long enough" bombarded the people twenty-four hours a day from the press, the radio, billboards, and sides of buildings. Every time they moved or turned around or spoke to each other, they grasped the idea that they were a superior race. Under the hypnotic influence of this suggestion, strengthened by repeated suggestions, they started out to prove it.

They *thought* about it all day long. In their hearts they became "superior." We have heard that "as a man thinketh, in his heart, so is he."

This power of suggestion introduced them to pride. As they dwelled on pride, their hearts became filled with pride—the greatest sin of the spirit. Their hearts became hardened; they were rendered unteachable by the light of Christ—conscience—and thus, were able to murder!

The power of suggestion can also be a great and good tool. The famous coach Knute Rochne entered the locker room at half-time during a game his team was supposed to win. Over-confident and lacking spirit, they were losing miserably. He opened the door to the room, started to walk in, looked around and said, "Oh, excuse me, I thought this was the locker room of the famous Notre Dame football team!" Then he promptly turned around and left them. His team went out on the field and creamed their opponents in the second half of the game!

Every successful or wealthy business has understood the power of suggestion. Ideas, products, services—all are sold to a gullible public on the *suggestion* of what it can do for them!

In whatever way it's applied, the power of suggestion is definitely very real. Remember what Hitler said: in the hands of someone who knows how to use it, the law of suggestion is a terrible weapon!

Satan has been given this power. It is called the power to bruise our heels. And he knows how to use it! In his hands it is a terrible weapon. His bruising of our heels is more deadly than a black and blue mark. He simply suggests to us that we cannot overcome, indeed, we *need* not overcome our weaknesses. He simply *mentions* that we are incapable, unworthy, etc., and we end up believing him because we *choose* to think about his thoughts and suggestions.

But the greater power we have been given, the power to crush his head, is the *freedom of choice.* Negative and positive thinking are not attitudes, *they are choices!* You are the sum total of the thoughts you *choose* to think!

Day after day we hear the negative thoughts: times are hard, the economy is suffering, banks are failing, prosperity is gone for good, it's not safe after dark, etc.

We begin to *think* hard times and hard life!

Think about this: if people would stop *thinking* about depression and wars, they would cease to exist *because nothing can be created unless it first begins with a thought.*

All this talk about depression might be eliminated from our vocabulary and lives! Seminars should be held on positive thinking, not depression. Depression should not be an emotional crutch. I agree that there is such a thing as a chemical depression, but I am also aware and informed by many professional people in medicine and psychology that even the chemical depression is usually integrated with thoughts which generate it in the body, and that true chemical depression is rare in comparison to that sustained by thought processes.

Thinking proper thoughts can keep our spirits healthy.

One of my sisters suffers acutely with pre-menstrual syndrome. She has even been hospitalized because she is an extreme and severe case. Her body has suffered great physical stress. She has maintained a positive balance spiritually and has not been depressed through any of it. Her spirit is healthy; she is in tune. She has accepted this condition; it is just that, a condition. She has eternal perspective and has covenanted to bear her burdens patiently.

Another woman with a classic case of supposedly "chemical depression" told me that after a year of suffering, the spirit told her to get off the drugs and go to the temple. She did and has not been depressed since, because she is striving to keep her spirit healthy.

Another woman I know was attacked by a horrible virus that damaged her nerve tissue permanently. She said the doctors told her a chemical depression was inevitable, and she told them no, it was not. She "worked through" her condition and found the Holy Ghost to be her comforter and counselor. She has not experienced one depressed moment.

The apostle Paul used perfect words when he counseled us to "*Press* toward the mark for the prize of the high calling of God" (Philippians 3:14).

What is a press? Is it a gentle push? No, it is a great force of effort. The old physics principle applies here, too. Whenever there is a *press* in one direction, there is an equal *press against* .

When Paul told us to "press" toward the mark, he meant it,

because of the tremendous press of the adversary and of mortality in general *against us.* Whenever we stop our "press" or stop pressing forward, we "un-press" or "de-press." In other words *depress!* The counsel is for our *exact* knowledge.

Now consider the meaning of the word *Gethsemane.* It literally means "olive-press." An olive press is used to squeeze the oil from the olives. There in that garden, the greatest press ever known to mankind took place. So great was the Savior's *press* that he sweated blood from every pore. Is it not comfort and inspiration that he did not de-press in his excruciating and painful suffering?

Yes, we are subject to becoming discouraged and tired, but that is not depression. We must press forward to cheerfulness and new vigor in order to vanquish depression. Satan would discourage us, cause us to despair, because we can't accomplish if we have crippled thoughts! But it is our choice. *You decide* every morning if you are going to be happy or sad, positive or negative.

Every negative thought that Satan places in our mind, we choose to accept it, tolerate it, eventually to embrace and believe it, or to dispel and vanquish it! It is our choice. It wasn't given to our parents, mates, friends, neighbors or even our environment to be in charge of our thoughts. It's how *we* choose to see and think about things that determines our whole feeling about life.

I listened to two men discuss their ride into a large city from the suburbs each day. They took a public commuter train; the ride was about forty minutes. One of the men complained about the hassle, the crowds, the boredom, the monotony. The other man said he loved the time to collect his thoughts, watch the scenery, prepare his day, meditate. It was the same train, the same ride, the same scenery, but one man loved it, one man hated it. The difference was not in personality; the difference was in *choice.*

And so each of us will determine what power we will have in this life and the next by what we *choose* to think of ourselves. Again my favorite proverb, "You can't stop a robin from lighting in your hair, but you can keep him from building a nest there." We can't stop Satan from using his power of suggestion, but we can use the *power of choosing* to change those thoughts and not let them stay.

How is that possible? How is it done?

Cast Away Your Idle Thoughts

This means don't dwell on the "nothings." Whether it be the garbage Satan suggests to us, or the garbage of the world, we should *cast away* these thoughts. The television soap operas are a perfect example of idle thinking. So are gossip sessions, romance novels, and any form of light-mindedness.

Idle thoughts are also dwelling on past mistakes, tragedies, or hurt. Letting these idle thoughts fill our minds will eventually dull, even poison, the senses.

A woman called me recently and told me she wanted to die. She had contemplated taking her life, even how she was going to do it. She told me that she could not live another day with the horrible thoughts that crawled out of every dark corner in her mind.

Nearly an hour passed before I could persuade her to tell me the secrets and pain of those thoughts. Slowly, very slowly, she began to unfold a bitter and tragic story.

She had been sexually abused by her father from the time she was nine until fourteen years old. She had never told anyone, not even her husband. She lived with the fear of rejection, guilt, resentment, and sexual handicap. It was causing great stress in her marriage.

She said she struggled each year and kept hoping as the years went by that she could somehow tell him or somehow forget. But she was thirty-five now, and it seemed impossible to her to go on living anymore with the burden.

We talked long into the night. Finally, as I was about to hang up, I felt her fear rise again. She had committed to see her bishop and tell him. I had suggested that he would be able to help her tell her husband. Together they all three could find proper counsel and help for her. I knew she would be safe with her bishop.

But now I could feel she was afraid to hang up, afraid she wouldn't see the bishop. So I asked her, "What did you do today to change the past?"

A long silence and then she replied, "Nothing."

I said, "Nothing? Well, what did you do yesterday to change the past?"

Again she thought and replied, "Nothing."

I said, "Nothing at all? What did you do all last week, all last year?"

Again the answer was "Nothing."

Finally, I asked her what ideas she had that she could do to change what had happened in the past.

She answered, "I don't have any ideas. . . . Please, help me. What *can* I do to change the past?"

And I answered her, "Nothing." Another long silence, and I continued, "Sweetheart, there isn't one thing that you can do to change the past. What has happened has happened. It's over. What you can do is start dealing with today. How do you start doing that? By stop dwelling on the things that you can do nothing about."

This idea had not occurred to her before, and she was very intense in trying to understand. As we continued talking, she could clearly see that it might work and was willing to try.

Today she is *working* through her problems without dwelling on the past. She is changing the things she can and accepting the things she cannot change and seeking wisdom to know the difference.

For My Thoughts Are Not Your Thoughts

. . . neither are my ways your ways saith the Lord. . . . For as the heavens are higher than the earth, so are my ways higher than your ways and my thoughts than your thoughts (Isaiah 55:8-9).

We should not counsel the Lord. We shouldn't try to tell him what to do for us. We should work to increase our faith in him and understand that he does know our needs and also our wants. In perfect harmony he places us here on earth to experience things that will enable us to learn and grow, not to be crippled.

We shouldn't raise our fist to heaven and ask the question, "Why is this happening to me?" The Lord's timing is much better and much more perfect than ours because he has all the news, all the facts. Several years ago we built a large commercial building in which to house our interior design business and a retail home accessories store. It was prime property in a prime location. We experienced great success and continued to establish goals to build the business and work there for the rest of our lives. Then things started changing. We adopted our little girl Paige. My oldest son turned thirteen. The demand to speak and write to the women in the Church tripled. My husband wanted to expand his talents and go back to dental school. Suddenly I felt the dramatic pull between the helpless needs of an infant to the adult needs of a teenager. The two children in between, also far apart in age, each needed separate attention. My desire to serve also increased, and Steve enrolled at the local university to prepare for admission to dental school. The pressure was intense; the clients were demanding. The retail store needed attention, too.

The decision became obvious—sell the building. It was a decision not without turmoil, because all along everyone involved had not only believed but *felt* that building was the right thing to do.

We put it up for sale and asked for help in our prayers. The pressure kept mounting. In the next two years we received several offers, but they either fell through, or we didn't approve them. Finally, we sold the building in accordance with our desires and terms.

Looking back I now see clearly several things that looking forward I could not see at all. First, all the offers that fell through came from people who are now bankrupt or have quit business. At the time I thought the world was against us! I couldn't understand why our prayers weren't being heard. Weren't my desires to be home righteous desires? Of course, our prayers were being heard. It just wasn't time yet.

When I quit asking, "Why is this happening?" I began learning more about patience. I learned some things that I *needed* to know, things also necessary to prepare me for another trial yet to come that, of course, I knew nothing about.

Looking back now I also realize that selling the building was the way we were able to go to dental school. And it is also the means by which my dad and his wife will be able to go on their mission. Looking back, it is clear that these were the real purposes of the "future" for us.

We cannot know what lies ahead; we cannot understand God's

higher thoughts and ways. We must be patient and submissive and *think* about our Father's love for us and his desire to teach us correctly.

Take Therefore No Thought For The Morrow

This doesn't mean "eat, drink and be merry, for tomorrow we die." It doesn't mean we should not establish goals or plans. It means don't dwell on those things that are unseen or undone. Thomas Carlyle once wrote, "Our duty is not to *see* what lies dimly in the distance, but to *do* what clearly lies at hand."

One of the problems that makes us dwell on negative thoughts is our thirst for perfection. How many times have you done the right thing over and over and then suddenly slipped back and done the wrong thing? We want so much to be better, to do the right thing, to be perfect. But in our frail mortal existence we simply cannot be perfect in the total sense of perfection. Yesterday we took four steps forward, but today we take twelve backwards, and then we feel power-less!

Being perfect isn't at all important in mortality. Yes, the goal should be high. "Be ye therefore perfect even as your Father which is in Heaven is perfect." If the goal isn't high, if our reach doesn't exceed our grasp, we will never know all we can become. Buf if we had to wake up every morning and be perfect all day, how long do you think it would take before we would run for the razor blades! I can't deal with perfection like that. Certainly we can and must be perfect in specific ways, and we must not accept mediocrity as acceptable behavior. But being The Perfect Woman isn't at all important in mortality. Rather, *the consistency in striving for perfection* is what is important. Then perfection becomes the result of the behavior and not the behavior itself. For example, in your personal prayers, which is more important right now: to be inspired and perfect in every prayer or to be consistent in praying? If you try to rush out and be perfect in every prayer, you may succeed if you have no other responsibilities in life! However, most of us would encounter a day or a moment of extreme fatigue, self-concentration, stress, demands, distractions, etc., and find ourselves amiss in our prayers. If being perfect was to be instant, many would easily become discouraged and stop praying. Prayer is, like everything else, a process to be practiced and learned.

If, however, the goal is to be consistent in praying, then even if communication has not taken place, the simple act of obedience is ingrained. Eventually, through consistency, prayer becomes a part of routine and personal habit. As prayer is consistent, answers and communication come. Through consistency the person also practices understanding the language of the spirit. *Through consistency in striving for perfection* in prayer, the person becomes more and more perfected in communicating and listening. They would be "getting used to it."

We cannot let this idea of perfection leave us powerless as we worry about tomorrow. It is the "labor of a lifetime—and more."

Let Virtue Garnish Thy Thoughts Unceasingly

". . . then shall thy *confidence* wax strong. . . (D&C 121:45; emphasis added).

Strong, confident (virtue also means strength) thoughts develop from thinking and dwelling on strong, positive ideas. First we have to recognize the negative thoughts around us. We don't choose or not choose to have Satan place suggestions in our minds. That was the power given him to bruise our heels. We do not choose whether or not to have negative people, circumstances, or experiences come into our lives. They are ever with us. *We do choose what to do with them.*

Just like strength of muscles comes from exercising them, so does strength of mind come from exercising strong thoughts. In exercising your mind, first *picture* strong thoughts.

A sportswriter in the 1930s named Grant Rice liked to talk about the phenomenal amateur golf player John Montagu. Montagu reportedly could "run rings around anyone and place the ball precisely where he wanted it to land." Rice said the ball would go wherever Montagu wanted because he believed golf was really played with the *mind.* Montagu was quoted, ". . . Of course, there are fundamentals of stance, grip, swing, but I must have a clean, clear mental *picture* of what I am doing before I play the shot. That mental picture takes charge of the muscular reaction. If there is no mental picture, what happens is mere guess."

I have a friend who told me a similar story about her brother. They grew up in Malad, Idaho and were from an active LDS home. Everyone in the family liked school except this particular brother. He was failing miserably, even though he was an extremely bright boy. He had a track record as a poor student. He could not picture himself any other way.

A new school year began, and a wise and loving teacher taught him the power of picturing himself with strong thoughts. Again he was doing poorly. He was unattentive and apathetic about school in general. When the first report card came, much to his astonishment the teacher had given him straight A's! Of course, he hadn't earned them, but she told him that she knew he was a straight A student, and he might as well get used to the idea. For the first time in his life he could "picture" himself already there. From that moment on he never received anything lower than an A. Today he is a prominent and successful surgeon in Salt Lake City.

If you can't picture yourself in the celestial kingdom, how can you get there? It is important for us to develop eternal perspective. Perspective is being able to see things in terms of depth perception and/or overall view. The objects closest to us are larger than those far away. Children have a hard time understanding perspective. Their drawing usually depicts all objects about equal in size, proportion, and distance. They cannot capture on paper the reality of what they see.

People who get into spiritual trouble in this life have lost—even if temporarily—their *eternal* perspective. They are only seeing things in terms of "up close." It is a very "flat" perception of what life and existence truly is.

Eternal perspective for me has been the mental exercise to "picture" myself in a long white flowing gown of exquisite fabrics and laces, my face radiant, my hair glowing, standing in the midst of my brothers and sisters of heaven in the midst of the Savior and our heavenly parents. It is a great exercise and has saved me on occasion from making a wrong choice!

The second step to garnishing strong thoughts is to dwell or concentrate on our personal gifts and use them to help others. Right now make a list of all the things you like about yourself. Come on. It's a great way to discover real gifts about yourself. There is no such thing as false modesty here. If we can't recount to ourselves and the Lord the gifts he gave us, how can we use them or report our stewardship over them to him?

Third, develop a spirit of never quitting. Winston Churchill came to visit a group of school boys in Dover after heavy bombing and casualties in London. The boys had been prepared, having been told that Mr. Churchill was the greatest leader England ever had. They were encouraged to hang on to every detail and word he spoke because this was the chance of a lifetime for them.

Winston Churchill arrived on time and was escorted to the front of the class. All present expected a fiery and eloquent speech. He stood calm and quiet for a moment and then looked carefully into the face of each boy. His entire speech lasted thirty seconds, but it has long been remembered and still remains an inspiration. He said, "Never give up. Never give up! Never, never, never, NEVER give up!"

A lot of people know that Marian Anderson was the notable black singer with the gorgeous contralto voice. Yet few people even know of her humble background. She came from a Negro slum neighborhood and poor parents. There was never enough food, heat, or clothes. Education was minimal; the Negro was a second class citizen.

Marian wanted a violin when she was six years old and began scrubbing doorsteps in Philadelphia for five cents each. Later on in her youth she sang in her church, took in washing, ironing—which was hard, grueling work in those days—to pay for violin lessons and schooling.

Once she got her musical degree, she then faced the cruelty of being a black woman in a white, anti-black society. She was threatened, humiliated, and shunned. But she never gave up. She climbed slowly to world fame, literally climbing back stairways and entrances because whites were offended if she used the front door.

Her triumph is one of the most dramatic in musical history. It was in Washington, D.C. on Easter Sunday 1939 that this black woman of humble beginnings and great obstacles sang on the steps of the Lincoln Memorial. She thrilled 75,000 people there that morning—cabinet members, senators, congressmen, and famous people from business and society—because she never gave up!

Heed The Scriptures

> Cease to be idle; cease to be unclean; cease to find fault one with another; cease to sleep longer than is needful; retire to thy bed early that your bodies and minds may be invigorated (D&C 88:124).

What great ideas for positive thinking! What great advice on getting rid of negative thinking!

First he said *cease* negative behavior and thinking. Just stop doing it. It truly can be done overnight. It is possible. Try *replacing* the negative with the positive. *Cease to be idle.* A single divorced lady did absolutely nothing to better her lot in life. She moped and complained for years. She moved back in with her parents and waited to marry again. When she stopped being idle, she changed her life. Now back in school, she has new goals and is making good progress. She has *ceased* negative thinking.

Cease to be unclean. The spirit won't dwell in an unclean body or place. If he is not there, he can't strengthen or comfort you. It is a lot harder to think positively without him.

I met a woman from a small farming town in Central Utah. She had seen no reason to clean up her home, yard, or physical appearance. After meeting her and discussing this *basic* gospel concept she agreed to try and gain a testimony of it. Six months later she wrote:

> The first place I started was with myself. I bathed every day and kept my hair fixed up. I made a goal to put clean clothes on fresh each day. I even tried make up.
>
> At first I felt ridiculous going out to feed the pigs and work the garden in my makeup and clean hair and clothes.

But after just one week I tried to go back to my other way and just couldn't. I realized I actually did feel better!

The next thing I noticed was my husband. He liked it. He wanted to take me to town and get a new dress. He started fixing up, too. Then the kids started looking better. Pretty soon we got the house in order.

The yard was a big chore, but we all liked the clean smells. We sure liked being able to find things. . . .
I guess I'm trying to saying we've been a lot happier since we've been cleaner.

Cease to find fault with one another. How we view others is really how we see ourselves. As we judge the behavior of others, we judge it according to our knowledge, *not of them,* but of ourselves. Usually we see other people doing things in reference to the way we would do things.

It's not right to criticize, backbite, and gossip. What is it we are really saying? We are really saying, "I don't feel good about myself, so I need to put someone else down."

Several years ago a woman wrote to me who had the opportunity of an interesting lesson in fault-finding. She wrote:

There is a woman in my ward consumed with looking for the faults of others. It has been my experience to witness how this nearly divided our ward. The contention became intense. Everyone suspected everyone else of harboring ill feelings. This woman judged others harshly and continuously, even in front of the congregation. I watched how this kind of behavior slowly ate away positive thinking and positive behavior. The process was so slow that damage was done before the bishop was aware what was happening.

One day he called me into his office, "Sue, there is a problem you need to take care of."

I knew that I had not escaped the evil gossip but had tried to ignore it, thinking it would all pass. The old expression "It takes both your enemies and friends to carry you the sting of life—your enemies to say it about you and your friends to carry the news" was so true.

The bishop went on to say that this woman had been coming in his office wanting me released as a teacher in Relief Society. He had tried to be tolerant and counseled against such feelings, but he felt she wasn't listening. The day he finally called me was to tell me that the woman had come in shouting, "Now I have the evidence I need to get Sue released!"

The "evidence" was a story told by this woman's home teacher. Apparently years before he had a business encounter with Sue that left him with the impression she was the kind that "would go for the throat." The bishop refused to listen to the story. He asked Sue to help him stop the wave of pus and evil speaking that was consuming the ward. "Go to them and make peace." She continued in her letter:

I was upset. Why should I make peace? I had done nothing. I had not participated in the vicious attacks on ward members. I hadn't even justified myself to ward members or "lined" up sympathetic supporters. As I thought longer and prayed about it, I realized that negative behavior can only be stopped with positive behavior.

The first thing I did was to visit the woman who was causing the problem. I approached the home and was invited in. I didn't accuse or defend; I simply said that I was afraid I had offended her and wanted her forgiveness. I didn't know what I had done, it was unintentional, but I was sorry.

Then I visited the home teacher, who at first professed ignorance. I told him I was there to beg his forgiveness for offending him long ago. Would he please tell me what I did so I could make amends?

Finally, he admitted he had spoken unkindly and said, "Well, I guess I'd better practice that old principle that says if you can't say anything good about anybody, don't say anything at all."

I leaned over my chair and looked him eye to eye and said, "Oh, no, my friend, that's not the principle at all. The Lord's principle is: *if you don't have anything good to say about anybody, get RID of those feelings.*

Cease to sleep longer than is needful. When we sleep too much, we become guilt ridden and even more despondent and negative over things undone. If we oversleep, often our whole day is out of "synch." The rest of the counsel is "retire early" or in other words, don't knock ourselves out. Getting the proper rest leaves our minds clear and free to think and sort through our decisions. Tired, weary minds are perfect beds of soil for Satan's weeds of negative thinking.

We can't ever forget who is (or isn't) in charge and in control of our minds! We are! We must not forget all those precious gifts the Lord has given us. Surely the most precious gift the Lord has given us is the freedom to choose for ourselves. Positive thinking is a choice we must make.

The bumblebee is not supposed to fly. By all laws of aerodynamics its body is too big for its wings. But the bumblebee doesn't know that. So it flies!

Chapter Four

The Power to Make Things Happen

CHARLES SCHULTZ is the wise and witty creator of the Peanuts comic strips. One of his well-known classics depicts Lucy asking Charlie Brown, "What is your favorite day, Charlie Brown?" To which he replies, "I'm sort of fond of tomorrow."

Me, too!

Tomorrow holds new possibilities, new adventures. Tomorrow is filled with opportunity and mystery. Somehow tomorrow holds promises of rewards and promises of surprise.

But, all too often, tomorrow can be our worst enemy. Tomorrow can be the seductive thief of our time called procrastination. Why do we procrastinate?

The quickest reply is well, we are lazy. This might be true in a lot of mundane chores we do, but almost everyone reading this book wants to accomplish, yearns to improve, wants to do what's right. You are right here reading this today because you want to make things happen!

There are other reasons we don't get things done. Perhaps you can find others, but there are four that I have experienced at one time or another in my life.

1. You aren't used to accomplishing regularly and feel overwhelmed at the task at hand.
2. You don't really believe you can do it and so, choose

not to try.

3. You are afraid of failing or facing the fact you've failed. You think you won't do a good enough job.

4. You take on too much and try to be too many things to too many people too much of the time.

I shall never grow tired of President Kimball's little motto: "DO IT!" When we procrastinate, we slow our progress; we don't make things happen as they should. Let's look carefully at the solutions to the other reasons we impede our growth.

You're Not Used To Accomplishing Regularly

"Thou shouldst set in order the things that are wanting" (Titus 1:5).

The Lord commanded us to "Organize yourselves and prepare every needful thing" (D&C 88:119) because without being organized we cannot accomplish regularly. When we are disorganized, or our lives and properties are not in order, we have the overwhelming feeling that life is controlling us.

What is truly being organized to the Lord? All of our lives we are taught to be organized by filing this, having a notebook for that, using special boxes, drawers, shelves, file cabinets, and etc. It appears that if we layer more things upon ourselves, we seem organized. But this is not organization to the Lord. His way is not a "layering" but an "unlayering," or *unburdening*, not adding to our burdens.

In a previous chapter I described my sister's experience with the first photograph of a living human embryo. We talked about how that embryo possessed everything it needed to become an adult human being. Then we likened it to us as Gods in embryo and that we don't go through life "finding" Godlike attributes, that they already exist within each of us. Through *divine heredity* we possess *all* that God possesses to become like him.

We aren't going to go through mortality finding patience, buying mercy, picking up charity. They are already within us. Rather, as we "unlayer" or "unburden" ourselves of weaknesses, there is more room available for these God-inherited attributes to develop. In getting rid of our weaknesses, we allow inner qualities to blossom.

Getting rid of "pretend" roles, old projects, discarded items in our lives, physical or emotional, is indeed being organized. We need the freedom to think and move spiritually in an unspiritual world! For example: If we have a problem with gossiping, we begin to "unlayer" by refusing to *say* anything evil about anyone. Now, after working on that for a few years, we become aware of yet another layer to remove, and we decide not to *listen* to any more gossip. A few years go by, and we see still another layer to peel off: we decide not to *think* bad thoughts about anyone. A few more years working on that, and we can see still another layer: we decide to *look* for the good in others. Getting rid of weakness allows the inner *inherited* God-given qualities to develop.

Organizing ourselves in our environments is precisely the same process. If we can discard old clothes, old projects, old possessions, useless tools and appliances, forgotten recipes, and so on, we can unclutter our homes and our thoughts. My sister went through her house and eliminated all of her "guilt trips," projects never finished that never would be, all those gadgets she never used but thought she'd get to someday but knew she never would. (She carried some things back and forth to the trash many times in an internal debate until they finally ended in the trash.)

Often I have to make my clients stop and evaluate their lifestyle and personal choices when planning their home decor. Somehow, especially when we move higher and higher socially and economically, we often perceive ourselves in the middle of an illusion. Many women *think* they want such an extreme change from their present environment, almost totally unsuited to their personalities. They somehow believe if they "live in it," they will "live like that." I always ask them to answer truthfully if they really believe they will walk around all day in a long flowing hostess gown.

My experience has been that when people do not plan or decorate their homes the way they live, they are never comfortable in them. They have "layered" upon themselves more work, more worry, more expense, more maintenance, than they ever really wanted. We do that with gadgets, clothes, even recipes, and many more things.

In her book, *Gift From the Sea*, Anne Morrow Lindbergh discusses this kind of organizing through "unlayering" or "getting rid of." She wrote this little book while on vacation at the beach:

> One learns first of all in beach living, the art of shedding . . . physical shedding to begin with, which then mysteriously spreads into other fields. Clothes, first. Of course, one needs less in the sun. But one needs less anyway, one finds suddenly. One does not need a closet full, only a small suitcase full. And what a relief it is! Less taking up and down of hems, less mending . . . less worry about what to wear. One finds one is shedding not only clothes—but vanity.
>
> Next, shelter. . . . Here I live in a bare sea-shell of a cottage. No heat, no telephone, no plumbing to speak of, no hot water, no gadgets, no rugs. There were some, but I rolled them up the first day; it is easier to sweep the sand off a bare floor. But I find I don't bustle about with *unnecessary* sweeping and cleaning here. . . . I have shed my Puritan conscience about absolute cleanliness. Is it possible that, too, is a material burden? No curtains. I do not need them for privacy; I want the windows open all the time . . . washable slipcovers, faded and old—I hardly see them! I don't worry about the impression I make on other people. I am shedding pride. As little furniture as possible; I shall not need much. . . . I find I am shedding hypocrisy in human relationships. What a rest that will be! The most exhausting thing in life, I have discovered, is being insincere. That is why so much of social life is exhausting; one is wearing a mask. I have shed my mask (Anne Morrow Lindbergh, *Gift from the Sea* [New York City: Pantheon Books], pg. 30-32).

Another tool for accomplishing regularly is to have priorities. How can you meet a goal if it isn't a priority? How can you get to the celestial kingdom if it isn't a priority?

Priorities need to be individual and flexible. Never, never plan your priorities as someone else, only plan them for YOU. Start out simply with a list of what you want to accomplish each day in the order of importance. Maybe your list would read like this:

Pray
Scriptures
Exercise
Make breakfast: family prayer
Car pool
Dry cleaners
Make Jello
Write note to Sister Jones
Temple session
Make dinner
Take Jello to Byrne's house
Family Prayer

Lists are meant to serve you, not you them, so when an unforeseen priority comes up, be flexible. As you become fluent in the purpose and importance of priorities you may want to schedule your time more exacting. Either way it doesn't matter, just so you are accomplishing.

Marie Curie, co-discoverer of radium, knew the importance of priorities in accomplishing regularly. As you read about her life, the conclusion is an obvious one. She made up her mind since her girlhood to become a scientist. It was a priority. She lived her life and made things happen by having a list of priorities.

When she was refused permission to study science at the University of Cracow because they believed girls should only study cooking, etc., she went to Paris and entered the Sorbonne. It was there that she met Pierre Curie, and together they set upon the task of tracking down at least one source of radioactivity. She had two daughters, a household to manage, ill health, and hours and hours of laboratory work. She never would have made it without priorities. Few women have been so greatly honored as Madam Curie, not only as a scientist and for her contributions in the world of science, but also as a wife, a mother, and a woman!

You Don't Believe You Can Do It—So You Don't Try
For behold, it is not meet that I should command in all things; for he that is compelled in all things, the same is a slothful and not a wise servant; wherefore he receiveth no reward.

Verily I say, men should be anxiously engaged in a good cause, and do many things of their own free will, and bring to pass much righteousness;

For the power is in them, wherein they are agents unto themselves. And inasmuch as men do good they shall in nowise lose their reward (D&C 58:26-28).

We *can* believe in ourselves. It's a choice. But first we must believe in God and that he is our Father, loves us, cares for us, and has put us here to prove to ourselves we are worthy of higher responsibilities in the world to come.

Joseph Smith taught that if we do not comprehend the character of God, we cannot comprehend ourselves. How can we trust ourselves if we cannot trust God? How can we love ourselves if we don't love God? How can we believe in ourselves if we don't believe in his love for us and his intentions for us? The Lord said the *power* is in us to make things happen. It is our choice to believe him or not to believe him. I believe him!

Guadalupe was one woman who chose to believe that in her was the power to make things happen.

Guadalupe Quintanilla was born in a small village in Mexico. Her parents divorced, and she was raised by poor but loving grandparents. When she was thirteen, she was sent to her father in Brownsville.

He immediately enrolled Lupita in school. When she scored poorly on an intelligence test given in English, she was placed in the first grade, the oldest child in the class. In school she did nothing more than hang posters and papers on the walls, and escort the younger girls to the washroom. She felt miserable, humiliated. After four months, she tearfully begged her father to allow her to drop out, and he reluctantly consented.

At sixteen, she married a Mexican-American dental technician. Within five years she had three children, two boys and a girl.

Lupita couldn't stand it when her boys were labeled slow. She knew they were bright, but without her help they wouldn't get the chance in life they deserved.

She had to learn English: spelling, grammar, pronunciation. She needed knowledge so that she could deal with the questions that troubled her children.

Lupita tried to read and understand their schoolbooks. A dictionary helped, but her progress was frustratingly slow. "It was no good. I needed to be taught."

Lupita had been working as a hospital volunteer, delivering flowers and mail to patients. She asked about the nurse's aide training program. The courses, taught in English, would force her to communicate in English. Impossible, she was told: a trainee must have a high school diploma.

She didn't know of an English course taught at night for adult Mexican-Americans, so she asked a high school counselor if she could sit in on a freshman English class. She vividly remembers the response: "Your records show you to be mentally retarded. I can't recommend your admission."

Lupita was crushed. Crying, she walked through the rain to her home. DON'T GIVE UP, she kept telling herself.

She again consulted her children's elementary-school principal, and together they reviewed the roadblocks. To her astonishment, the principal suggested trying Brownsville's Texas Southmost College, a two-year institution.

Lupita had to take two buses to get to the college. Without a high school diploma she couldn't get past the clerk in the registrar's office, but a student pointed out the registrar's car in the parking lot. She waited nearly two hours for him.

Impressed by Lupita's intensity, he promised to admit her to four basic courses. "However," he warned, "if you don't pass them, you're out."

Her family accepted her new pursuit. "I think my family assumed that I'd give up school after a short time and settle down at home again."

Lupita proved to be a fast learner. She awoke at 4:00 to do her homework and made the dean's list in her first semester. She then greatly increased her credit load.

By the end of her first college year, Lupita had discovered an exciting new world of knowledge and skills. She was astonished to realize that she now wanted a university degree. She enrolled in Pan American University in Edinburg, seventy miles from Brownsville, carpooling to the university on Tuesdays and Thursdays. She continued to attend Texas Southmost on Mondays, Wednesdays and Fridays. After three years, she had received both her junior-college degree and a Bachelor of Science degree, cum laude, from Pan American.

The children knew that she was different. Mexican-American mothers didn't attend college. Their love for her took on a new dimension; they admired her. Their mother was SMART. And as their own abilities improved with their mother's encouragement, so too did the boys' grades and self-confidence. They were moved to regular classes.

After graduation Lupita decided to take her children to Houston where her father now lived and where she could study Spanish literature at the University of Houston. Eager for more knowledge, she soon decided to go for a master's degree in Spanish literature.

Money was a problem. Small fees were made grading exams and working as a teaching fellow.

In 1971 Guadalupe Quintanilla received her Master of Arts in Spanish literature. When the university launched a new program of Mexican-American studies, she was offered the post of interim director. "I don't want an interim post," she replied. "If I'm going to take the headaches of a new program, I want to cure those headaches." Lupita was named permanent director.

Although she knew nothing about administration, as always, she learned fast. Her new challenges prompted her to go for a doctorate in education.

But she never slighted her children. She juggled her schedule to dash home and greet them after school. She went to the school parents' evenings and attended all the sports events in which her children participated.

In 1977, after earning her doctorate, Lupita received a one-year fellowship from the prestigious American Council on Education. She also was the first Hispanic woman winner in the history of the awards.

After serving her fellowship at the University of Houston as an administrative intern in the office of the chancellor, she then was appointed assistant provost for undergraduate affairs and, in 1981, was promoted to assistant provost of the 31,000-student university.

Seven and a half years ago Lupita read a newspaper report about a Chicago fire in which Hispanics died because they did not understand the firefighter's escape instructions, shouted to them in English.

Lupita offered to set up a Spanish-language course specifically designed for the police and firefighters.

The police, and later the fire department, agreed to her proposals. She also was hired to teach a course in ethnic relations at the police academy. Militant Hispanics castigated her for working with the police. To them, she was a tio taco, a Chicano expression meaning an Uncle Tom. She received threats to her life and obscene phone calls.

But she was convinced of the need for her program. Get the police to learn some street Spanish, she argued, and you'll reduce tension and conflict. "In itself, teaching a language is no big thing," says Lupita. "What we are really teaching is human awareness."

About 1400 police and firefighters have taken Lupita's Houston program, which has received praise from FBI training officers. President Reagan appointed her to the National Institute of Justice Advisory Board, which keeps the White House informed of new procedures and techniques in law enforcement, criminal justice and corrections.

This appointment is one of many honors heaped on Lupita. Others include: the Teaching Excellence Award from the University of Houston, the Quintanilla Scholarship Fund dedicated to her by a local Hispanic newspaper, the Outstanding Educator Award from Mexico's Autonomous University of Guadalajara.

These honors mean much to Lupita, but nothing goes deeper to her heart than the love of her children. Mario is now a physician, Victor a lawyer, and Martha a law student. Says Mario, "If we have done well, it is because she has given us the love, the confidence, and the support that enabled us to do well. I feel that God has touched me, and my mother was his hand" (Mario Quintanilla, "I Feel That God Has Touched Me, and My Mother Was His Hand, *Reader's Digest,* June 1984).

You Are Afraid of Failing or Facing Failure

Wherefore, as ye are agents, ye are on the Lord's errand; and whatever ye do according to the will of the Lord is the Lord's business.

And he hath set you to provide for his saints in these last days that they may obtain an inheritance in the land of Zion.

And behold, I, the Lord, declare unto you, and my words are sure and shall not fail, that they shall obtain it.

But all things must come to pass in their time.

Wherefore, be not weary in well-doing, for ye are laying the foundation of a great work. And out of small things proceedeth that which is great.

Behold, the Lord requireth the heart and a willing mind; and the willing and obedient shall eat the good of the land of Zion in these last days (D&C 64:29-34).

The Lord needs us to help him get the work done. He can't get it done without us. Oh, sure, we're going to have failures. We're humans, not Gods. But it's the little day-to-day tidbits of living that equal the grandeur of life. Failing and succeeding is life. All things—including failure—have place in our existence and learning. Out of small things proceedeth that which is great. All the Lord requires of us is a willing heart and mind, not perfection. Out of small effort comes great character—JUST TRY. There is nothing wrong with failing. But it is a horrible thing never to try because you are afraid of failing. The Lord said his words are sure and shall not fail. They shall not fail *us!*

As we read his scriptures, they are laced with expectation for us, love for us, patience for us, and support.

Henry Ford said:

One of the greatest discoveries a person makes, one of his greatest surprises is to find he *can* do what he was afraid to do! Most of the barriers we beat against are in ourselves.

If you watched any of the Los Angeles 1984 Summer Olympics, you saw athletes of a seasoned nature. How many do you think breezed their way to the top? Not one. They all experienced failure after failure after failure. Millions watched Mary Decker being tripped by another participant. She fell out of the way so as not to impede any other runners, and she was hurt. Her first reactions were bitter and tearful, but within hours she gained her composure and said her objective was to mend her leg and run *again.* And run and run and run until she tasted victory *again!*

J.C. Penney, the great department store tycoon, experienced bankruptcy early in his career. But he picked himself up and the next time tried harder. He never labeled himself a failure; he only *knew* he failed.

Albert Einstein had dyslexia. He was labeled slow and stupid by his teachers. He passed very few exams and had horrible grades. One of the genius minds of the world's history never considered himself a failure; he realized he only had *experienced* failure.

And President Spencer W. Kimball experienced many failures in his life. But he knew he wasn't a failure. Certainly the Lord wouldn't call a failure to be a prophet.

We are not *worthless* if we have failures and weaknesses; we are *worth less* to ourselves if we let them negatively defeat us instead of positively inspire us. Notice the difference between the attitudes of a woman who says: "I have failed several times," and the one who says: "I am a failure."

Let me tell you about my friend Alonna. She and her husband were the kind of couple that everyone oohed and ahhed over. He was a returned missionary and a tall, handsome loving husband. She was equally as beautiful and loving. Everyone was so impressed with their good looks and great relationship.

Years passed, and her husband became involved with the wrong kind of people at work. He began to fall away from church activity. Then he began to drink and take drugs. Finally he was under the control of alcohol and would even disappear for a week or two at a time while he was drinking. He also was unfaithful.

She felt like she had failed. Through the years she had tried to be an example. She had tried to help him, to rehabilitate him. She had tried to get church members involved in helping him, but he had refused.

Finally, she went to the Lord for help. After making a painful decision and receiving confirmation that it was right, she divorced her husband, left him and all his material possessions. She took her son and moved in with her parents.

Alonna didn't waste time feeling like a failure or saying, "I don't have any self-esteem because I am a failure." She was honest with herself, yes, but she took charge of her life.

She taught school for a year or so and saved enough to move to Arizona to pursue a master's degree. She simply said the marriage had failed, and now she needed to get on with her life.

She moved from Idaho to Phoenix and enrolled at ASU. It was not at all easy. She held down a part-time job, fulfilled duties for a grant, studied, raised her son, and somehow made ends meet. She was far away from family and friends. Yet cheerful and determined, she wanted to prove to herself she could meet her potential.

She did just that! She graduated this year and also remarried a wonderful man in the Mesa Temple. She, like all of us, has failed in her life, but she is in no way a failure!

You Take On Too Much

You try to be all things to all people all the time. "Do not run faster or labor more than you have strength and means" (D&C 10:4).

> To every thing there is a season, and a time to every purpose under the heaven:
> A time to be born, and a time to die; a time to plant, and a time to pluck up that which is planted;
> A time to kill, and a time to heal; a time to break down, and a time to build up;
> A time to weep and a time to laugh; a time to mourn, and a time to dance;
> A time to cast away stones, and a time to gather stones together; a time to embrace, and a time to refrain from embracing;
> A time to get, and a time to lose; a time to keep, and a time to cast away;
> A time to rend, and a time to sew; a time to keep silence, and a time to speak (Ecclesiastes 3:1-7).

We *cannot* be all things to all people all of the time. We search for outward simplicity because the inward simplicity (shedding or unlayering) is familiar to us and divinely inspired. But the world point of view is one of tension, conflict, and suffering; and we cannot escape this. There will never be an outward simplicity.

Our lives cannot implement in action the demands of all the people to whom our hearts respond. We can't marry them all or bear them all as children or care for them as we would our aging parents. We cannot read and digest all intellectual information on every moral subject, political platform, or historical moment. What we can do is to study out our priorities, chart a course of righteousness, and take time to refuel our wells.

My personal prayers have changed in the recent years from "Help me to be a good mother; inspire me in ways to meet my children's needs, to "inspire me *which child* needs me the *most* today."

The Savior left us with perfect examples of a time and season for all things, including refueling ourselves. If anybody could have been all things to all people all of the time, he could have. But he *wasn't*.

At age twelve when Mary and Joseph found him in the temple conversing with the Elders, he knew that was the time to be "about his father's business."

When Mary sat at his feet and Martha scurried in the other room to prepare food, he spoke of a time to learn. When he put aside the rebuke of his apostles because of the many people who wanted him, he took time to have the little children come unto him and play with him. There was a time to set things in order as he drove the moneychangers from the temple. He counseled about times *not* to preach and said don't cast your pearls before swine. There was a time to refresh and to eat when he broke the fishes and loaves for the multitudes. In Gethsemane he showed us there is a time to pray. And in front of Pilate, he knew it was the time to be silent. And as he hung upon the cross at Calvary, he demonstrated a time to forgive.

Each day we live brings "a time" to do many things. But unless we use wisdom and take time to refresh ourselves spiritually and emotionally, we will feel time is our enemy.

> Marilyn had a job—
> Working out her salvation.
> It wasn't 9 to 5.
> It was 9 to 9
> In 24-hour shifts.
>
> And there was no vacation, . . .
>
> She didn't have much fun
> On the job.
> It was more the retirement
> Benefits she was there for
> The mansion, the Glory.

On a typical day
She ran frantically
From the visual aid department
To the wheat-grinding and quilting department
To the grow your own
Vegetable department
And the sew your own children's clothing department
And the physical fitness department.

She even stopped running
Past the genealogy department
And locked herself in
Until she got something done,

And then she ran to the food
Storage department,
Ran with scriptures on cassette in hand.
Ran because there were 22-minutes left to fill,

"Urgent to Marilyn;
Peace, *be still*."

("Urgent to Marilyn," by Carol Lynn Pearson, *A Widening View* [Salt Lake City: Bookcraft], pp. 20-21.)

We must take time to reflect upon our senses. Do something for your sense of taste, touch, smell, sight, and hearing. Get in touch with the beautiful things around you. Relax. Enjoy some time to rest.

Myths

There are some myths that prevent people from changing their lives and making things happen. I firmly believe these myths have their roots from Satan.

It takes a long time to change. This is not true; many people change overnight. It doesn't make any difference how long you've been the way you are; you can change overnight if you're willing to make an effort. When the *heart* is changed, the behavior is changed. This can happen overnight.

Unless you know what motivates your behavior, you can't change it.

Another misconception. Many millions of experiences go into the development of your personality. Searching for a particular reason for particular behavior is like searching for needles in haystacks. What does it really matter?

If you're older, it's too late to change. Nonsense. Your behavior is not poured in concrete. Years do condition us, but the spirit is a lot older than the body. The spirit can change. Satan would have us believe our behavior is so ingrained we can't change. The Savior teaches that we certainly can change if we follow him.

If you change quickly, it won't last. Again wrong. Read the Book of Mormon and see account after account of people who "experienced the mighty change in their hearts" and were changed overnight. Look at King Lamoni and his wife. It was almost instant change, not even overnight. All someone needs to do is remove pride and let the spirit teach. All you need to do to change is to experience the change of spirit in your heart first and then adopt a new way of behaving.

It's almost impossible to change. Again, not true. Nobody is beyond change, or the Savior came in vain. All that you need to do is take the steps that will start the change process.

This is a note I received from a sweet and very spiritual young friend of mine. Her husband was excommunicated a few years ago:

Dear Anita:

This is part of a letter I was asked to write to the Stake President as part of Bob's coming back into the Church. I couldn't write a letter to a non-descript person so I addressed it to Bob.

... Two years ago in May, everything seemed to crash around me. I recall very distinctly the night you sat me down and told me what was happening with you, your life, the bishop, and the court. I was prepared to hear something drastic and prepared to listen without negative or positive emotion so I would not be a detriment to what was taking place in your heart. But even so, I was not prepared to hear what you had to say. I had to try with everything I possessed to keep a neutral face and reaction.

I remember my mind racing with confusion and unbelief.

When you were finished and I had asked some questions, I asked if I could leave for a while to clear my mind and sort through what had been said. I left and not until thirty or forty minutes later did I really realize what had taken place. . . . I needed someone to talk to . . . I could only think of your dad as you told me that you had talked with him. He was expecting my call. We talked for a while and questioned back and forth. I told him I was determined not to hold anything against you, not to despise or hate you, not to stand against you. . . . I told him this, but I told him I wanted to take care of and rectify any of those negative thoughts and feelings "NOW"! He kept telling me it would take time and time alone. I disagreed. If it was my position to forgive, I wanted that forgiveness to be complete, sincere, honest, and now! After leaving your father, I spent a little more time alone and a little more time in prayer and contemplation. Before I returned home, the negative thoughts and feelings were gone. . . .

Yes, Anita, I definitely agree IT DOES NOT TAKE A LONG TIME TO CHANGE. In fact, a change of heart like Alma talks about can come immediately if it is desired enough. Also, forgiveness or change or expulsion of the negative thoughts and feelings can last. It's not true that IF YOU CHANGE QUICKLY, IT WON'T LAST. Yes, negative feelings and thoughts would creep into my mind over the past two or three years, but just as quickly as they came in, I forced them out again. Only occasionally would I dwell on them and then realize what I was doing and get rid of them.

Recently a brother in our ward came to visit Steve and me for some comfort and advice. He and his wife had been having marital problems, and she finally went to see a lawyer. She could no longer live with his verbal abuse of her and the children. Although he had never hit her, his words had been just like hard-hitting blows.

He loved his family and wanted to make things right and had been willing over the past several years to go to counseling with her. But as he sat in our living room, facing this divorce, it became obvious that he had been trying to change *externally* and not internally. The result had been very little progress. The appalling discovery was that in his counseling sessions, he had been told that he was an abuser, and abusers can never change that about themselves. All they can do is learn to control themselves! My husband said, "If that is true, then what you are saying is that there are Gods out there in the universe who are abusers but just have it under control!"

This kind of thinking is meant to stop us from making things happen, to stop us from believing in ourselves, to stop the work of Jesus Christ.

It is probably not the prophet who will change your life, but those who have the one-on-one influence over you, those who understand the power of making things happen. Those who have influenced me have been those kinds of people. The spiritual leaders in the scriptures were clearly acquainted with the power in *making things happen* and how that power works in righteous influence over others.

> And it came to pass that I, Nephi, said unto my father: I will go and do the things which the Lord hath commanded for I know that the Lord giveth no commandments unto the children of men, save he shall prepare a way for them that they may accomplish the thing which he commandeth them (1 Nephi 7:9).

Nephi said, "Go and do it." President Kimball said, "Do it, now."

Chapter  Five

The Power in Having Courage

WORDS LIKE *pioneers, explorers, pilgrims, astronauts, frontiersmen* are all synonymous with journeys of adventure and courage. Always there has been courage in making a journey. Throughout the Lord's history of the Earth he has provided us with a symbol of our personal journey from the pre-existence to eternal life. In similitude he has led groups of people from one place of existence through a wilderness or through a journey of great difficulty, to a promised land.

Noah, Moses, Joshua, Lehi, Brigham Young, and others made journeys in similitude of our journey from the pre-existence through mortality, following our leader Jesus Christ, to the promised eternal life.

Their journeys weren't easy ones. They were filled with trial and dependence on the Lord. This journey through mortality is also filled with adventure, danger, and courage to rely with dependence on the Lord.

Some explorers and pioneers in history have sailed, driven, motored, or flown in their destinations. Theirs were, of course, physical journeys; ours is more of a spiritual journey.

We cannot fly to our destination. Have you ever taken an airplane? Yes, you get there faster, but you miss the scenery; you miss vital information about points of unique interest. And there is a danger. You could find yourself in a holding pattern, circling for hours because of heavy traffic. There is a danger you could be delayed or miss a connecting flight.

We cannot drive or be driven to our destination. All of us have taken a trip by car somewhere. Yes, we can see the scenery and stop at our leisure to enjoy points of interest. But sometimes we get distracted by the noise around us. In a new city we can get lost and waste valuable time trying to find our way. Then the real danger comes if the car breaks down, and we must depend on strange mechanics to repair it. Repairs can be costly and delay our journey.

We cannot go by train, either. Oh, yes, if the train breaks down, there is guaranteed repair, and we can still see the scenery. However, all we can really see is what is on either side of the train tracks. There is *no* chance to choose what we want to see. We are governed by the train company. And the danger is that we may fall asleep and not hear our destination announced, or we may become distracted by the crowds around us and not understand our destination.

We cannot sail through mortality, either. Taking a cruise sounds wonderful: big ocean liners filled with recreation, good food, and gratification for every whim. Oh, yes, it could be a relaxing way to get to our destination. However, we would lose the opportunity to change our minds if we didn't like the activities on board. There would be no way to get off. With only the ocean all around, we may become bored and lazy. One danger is that we may grow sea sick. Another danger is that the ship may sink, and we may drown.

We weren't meant to spiritually fly, drive, be driven, or sail through mortality.

This is the Journey of Journeys!

We were meant to WALK every step of the way. It's a spiritual walk from the pre-existence to eternal life. Mortality is often a turbulent storm, a barren desert, a strange wilderness, a formidable mountain, a seemingly endless sky, a dark forest.

Sometimes we will spiritually walk with great strength, briskly against the winds of every season. Sometimes we just take small and determined steps. Sometimes we walk with someone; sometimes others walk with us. Often we crawl on hands and knees.

There are the briars and thorns and noxious weeds with which to contend. Rocks, sand, and pebbles get in our shoes and bruise our heels. We stub our toe, scrape our knees; our skin bleeds, our back aches. Sometimes we are sun-burned, sometimes chilled, and mostly we are weary of the walking.

But along this spiritual, less traveled road, we are able to do things not possible in any other way than by walking.

We can stop and look back at the distance we have come. We can pause to drink from another's well and taste of their pure spirit. We can rest on a mountain top and see the view of struggles from up there and feel the victory of having climbed higher. We can pick a desert flower of special gifts that has not been noticed before. We can sit by a gorgeous waterfall of spiritual revelation. We can frolic in the leaves of repented sins.

Even though the world presses in around us with faces everywhere, it is mostly a lonely walk. At least we tend to feel it is. But we are not really alone at all.

Was it in similitude that the Savior left the prison walls and carried his cross as he walked the hot, dusty, and unfriendly streets of Jerusalem?

It was the Walk of Walks!

Was it not a pattern for our living, as was every aspect and corner of his life? Should we not reflect on the solitude of his walk as we carry our own crosses through the hot, dusty, and unfriendly roads of mortality?

> The Lord is omnipotent, with all power to control our lives, save us pain, prevent all accidents, drive all planes, ships, and cars, feed us, protect us, save us from labor, effort, sickness, even death—if he will—but he will not. . . .
>
> We should be able to understand this, because we can realize how unwise it would be of us to shield our children from all effort, from disappointments, sorrows, and suffering. . . .
>
> If we looked at mortality as the whole of existence, then pain, sorrow, failure, and short life would be a calamity. But if we look on life as an eternal thing stretching far into the pre-earth past and on into the post-death eternal future, than all happenings may be put into

proper perspective (Spencer W. Kimball, *Tragedy or Destiny*).

Proper perspective! That is the secret we discussed earlier in this book. It is the secret to having courage to endure our trials and tribulations and to endure them *well*.

How do we gain perspective of suffering and sorrow and thus develop courage?

1.   He thanked God and took courage (Acts 28:15).

Count your blessings! Thank God for all your blessings. It really works! I had the opportunity to prove this principle to myself.

Recently our family went through some of the most trying experiences of our lives. In preparation for a move to California in order for my husband to pursue his career development, we met a wave of opposition. Had we not had a *confirmation* we should make this change in our lives and careers, we would have given up under the continued tribulation and stress. In fact, so many people said, "Aren't all these troubles telling you that you shouldn't go?" More than once we were tempted to agree!

But the confirmation had been there. We knew that what we were about to do was the next step. It was the next part of our preparation for life and service in the kingdom.

We put our house up for sale and almost immediately the trials began. Every job that we had in the business suddenly developed a major problem. Delays in shipping and back orders became more plentiful than completed orders. We had clients with serious deadlines that we had to meet. We did business with one client who proved to be the worst one we'd ever had. We lost valuable time in freight delays and mixups. There were problems I never want to go through again.

On top of all this we sold our house and had to be out in six weeks. We packed every spare minute. Sorting, throwing, packing, every waking moment at home. We ate off paper plates for one month.

Worse yet, we had plumbing problems again, and the drains were backed up in the showers, toilets, and sinks for days while the plumbers tried to fix the messes.

During this time my heaviest schedule of speaking assignments took me from home four weekends out of six. We were having problems with one of our children in school; we found out that a most loved and admired relative had been on marijuana. On top of all of this we had illness, Steve's exams, and other family problems. Then someone smashed the back of my car.

All during this time I had not once said, "Why me?" I had made up my mind that I would do as Elder Maxwell had counseled in one of his books. He suggested we follow Jesus' invitation to be of good cheer at the *outset* of our trials instead of crying and complaining, because we finally end up relying on good cheer anyway. Why not do it at the outset of problems and eliminate unneeded anxiety that stops our progress.

I had determined when these problems began to develop that I would try the Lord on this promise. I testify to you that it works! If it will work for me—an ordinary woman who hates trials and does my share of crying and complaining—then it will work for you, too!

With each trial, I smiled and pushed back the tears, never *allowing* even one to fall during those months of turmoil. I kept repeating over and over "Be of good cheer. I, the Lord am with thee and have not forsaken thee." It really worked! And then, two days before we were to close escrow on the sale of our house, the buyer disqualified himself, and the sale was cancelled.

During the next few hours of "darkness" I tried to grasp at the meaning of all this. Steve was to start school in four weeks; we knew that the decision to go back to school was right; we had received the confirmation by the spirit. The Lord knew everything we owned was in boxes, and I knew he knew our many other needs. As the doubts and questions started gathering, so did the black clouds of gloom. For the first time in three months, I didn't feel like being of good cheer at all!

But something in me wouldn't give up after all these months of success. I went into my room and started to write down my blessings. One by one I started counting them until the words turned into lines, and the lines turned into pages. By the time I was finished I was so overwhelmed at all the wonderful blessings the Lord had given me, no way could I be sad! How dare I?

Sisters, in my *weakness*, I testify to you that counting our blessings is one of the simplest things to do to have courage—and one of the most important! I testify to that scripture (Acts 28:15). It is true.

Within five days we had worked out all of our problems. As the answers came, we marvelled once again at the timing and wisdom of our Heavenly Father. All is well.

2. Therefore, now let your hands be strengthened, and be ye valiant (2 Samuel 2:7).

Courage is strengthened by being valiant in our testimony that Jesus is the Christ. How many times have we said, "I can't take it anymore. I've had enough!"

What if after three years of service without purse, shelter, or comfort, after suffering Gethsemane, the mockery, the trial, the beatings, the torture, the nails on the cross, what if the Savior had said, "I can't take anymore; I've had enough," and walked down off the cross?

It would have changed many things. All his example would have been for naught. We would have had no faith in those words. We would each have had to be crucified or sacrificed. The whole spiritual world would need to be restructured, regrouped.

But he didn't say that. Instead he was valiant. He hung there valiant in his love for us! Can we do any less for him?

A woman shared this story of understanding courage by being valiant in the testimony of Jesus Christ. She was training to be a nurse and was scheduled to do clinical time with terminal patients. She was to meet their psychological needs, as well as their physical needs. She was terrified. She didn't feel she could do it; she even made herself sick thinking about it. But she had to do it because her grade depended upon completing this assignment.

As she entered the hospital she wondered how she would ever discuss death with someone who was not LDS. She worried she would not feel peace in this task.

Once on the terminal patients floor, she glanced over the chart of Eve Crisp, her assigned patient. It said, "Eve Crisp. Terminal Cancer—final phase." In the corner of the chart under religious affiliation were the letters *LDS*.

Quickly I slipped into her darkened room. Her eyes dimmed by months of suffering brightened a bit as I took her hand in mine and introduced myself as Sister Cain.

We visited easily as I met her physical needs. I learned that my patient still had several children at home. She was only forty-seven years old. She spoke of the Church and a time that she had traveled to attend a general conference. It was one of her fondest memories. I mentioned the upcoming April conference broadcast that would be aired in part the following Sunday morning. She smiled.

Often during the day she would respond to the cries of a little boy down the hall who had been badly burned by saying, "Poor thing, he must be suffering so." Her sympathy and compassion seemed overwhelming for one suffering so much as herself. I marveled at her. The time came all too soon for me to leave. Before I left, I straightened her pillow and reached for her signal light on the bed sheet. As I placed it in her hand, she held on to mine and answered the question I was unable to ask.

"The Lord is perfect. His plan for me is perfect, and I know he loves me."

I embraced her and moved silently out into the corridor. I took a deep breath before returning to the main desk to make a notation on her chart. The notation read, "Please see to it that Mrs. Crisp's TV is tuned to the LDS general conference on Sunday morning at six o'clock." I then went to a report meeting and bore my testimony to a class of nonmembers that I could only hope would appreciate my remarks.

The following Monday, my supervising instructor called me from my class work into her office. I was told Sister Crisp had died that Sunday morning shortly after the television show she had been watching had ended. I shed tears for her that I would shed for no one else. She had taught me so much. "The Lord is perfect; his plan is perfect, and I know he loves me" (*Ensign*, August 1984, p. 67).

If we have faith enough to believe in the Savior and his love for us, it is *after* not *before* or *during*, but *after* the trial of our faith come the blessings. It is *through* our suffering we can really come to know the Master and prove we love him. Being valiant in our testimony increases our courage. "Be still and know that I am God."

3. *Bear* with patience thine afflictions (Alma 26:27).

What does *bear* mean? Those who have delivered children know the pain of that word, both in carrying and delivering the child.

All of us can understand that word *bear*; it means to carry the heavy load. Carry the cross with strength; it will never be one you'll have to be nailed to. Just *bear up* under the burden. *Bear down* against the forces of opposition. And bear affliction with *patience*. The Lord would not leave us abandoned. He only wants to see us strengthened.

Can I tell you about a woman I know who has indeed borne her afflictions with patience and long suffering. Her name is Judy. A few years ago she was driving home from the Manti Temple pageant when the brakes failed on her camper truck, and she went over the side off the road. The camper rolled over, and two of her three children—her six-year-old son and eight-year-old daughter—were crushed to death. Her oldest son almost died and had to be watched with guarded care for weeks after the accident. Judy *bore* the grief with dignity and with patience. She loves the Lord.

This incident was not her only affliction. Her husband had been somewhat inactive. She patiently loved and stood by him until he became reactivated. He had also suffered surgeries and illnesses and a brush with death. A new infant son almost drowned in their pool. Her oldest son nearly died this summer with a brain concussion. Her mother died unexpectedly last year. They have suffered financial pressures because of many medical bills. And I'm sure there are numerous other problems of which no one is even aware, because Judy never complains nor grows impatient with the Lord. She is *bearing* her afflictions with *power*. She is proving what power there is in courage.

I am becoming increasingly more aware of the necessity of patience in order to master ourselves and feel real power. Without patience as a *growing* characteristic in our lives, we are *power-less*. I think the *challenge* to us especially in these last days, is to develop a depth of patience in our lives. Our space age technology has made a journey of thousands of miles into mere hours; hours of laundering have now been reduced to hot cycle, warm wash, and cold rinse; harvest time is now the length of the line at the supermarket checkout counter; and we can bake a potato in six minutes. The computer will soon become as commonplace a household item as a television. I have a friend who has slowly realized her children have no real sense of the patience involved to work out their problems because of television. They watch problems solved in thirty minutes to an hour and figure their own problems are unsolvable if they can't be resolved in that kind of time frame.

The computerized space age lifestyle is teaching us to "hurry, hurry" and "it's not worth the wait!" Much of the advertising we hear is trying to tell us we shouldn't have to wait for anything. Without even realizing it, we are being geared to that impatient way of living. We need patience to improve our powers of courage.

4. Pray without ceasing (Alma 34:2).

If we don't pray continually to our Father and keep the network lines of communication open, then if we suddenly need to pray, it seems we are sending more of an S.O.S. than a prayer to heaven. Prayer is not for God; prayer is for *us*. He has all the news already. Prayer is for us to align ourselves to his will. He views us not from a position of indifference, but rather of one from love.

> He is not a passive God who merely watches lights on a cosmic computer and presses buttons to implement previously laid plans; he is a personal God, who is just, merciful, and kind. His great desire is not to count his creations like so many coins, but to bind up the broken hearts of the inhabitants of each world. Sanctification is his work! (Neal A. Maxwell, *Even As I Am*, p. 30).

As we learn to pray in our search for power in being courageous, it is important to pray *specifically*. To thank and ask and repent in *specifics* is what he wants us to do. Then he can answer and comfort and forgive us, *specifically*.

Imagine yourself as a living house. God comes in to rebuild that house. At first perhaps, you can understand what he is doing. He is getting the drains right and stopping the leaks in the roof, and so on. You knew that those jobs needed doing and so you are not surprised. But presently, he starts knocking the house about in a way that hurts abominably and does not seem to make any sense. What on earth is he up to? The explanation is that he is building quite a different house from the one you thought of—throwing out a new wing here, putting on an extra floor there, running up towers, making courtyards. You thought you were going to be made into a decent little cottage: but he is building a palace (C. S. Lewis, *Mere Christianity* [New York City: MacMillan, 1960], p. 174).

No, we can't fly, drive, sail, or even be driven to our final destination. It is a WALK we *must* make.

Yea, though I *walk* through the valley of the shadow of death, I will fear no evil: for thou art with me; thy rod and thy staff they comfort me (Psalms 23:4).

Oh, that my people had hearkened unto me, and Israel had *walked* in my ways! (Psalms 81:13)

Then Jesus said unto them, Yet a little while is the light with you. *Walk* while ye have the light, lest darkness come upon you (John 12:35).

For ye were sometimes darkness, but now are ye light in the Lord: *walk* as children of light: (Ephesians 5:8)

In the Doctrine and Covenants the Lord calls it *"a godly walk."* And that, it truly is: a walk to Godhood.

Chapter  Six

The Power of Love

YOU HAVE heard from me before the thought that if you could catch a vision of the woman God intends for you to become, you would rise up and never be the same again.

What is that vision? What does he intend for you, for each of us, to become? "Therefore what manner of [women] ought ye to be?" In other words, what do I *expect* you to become, *intend* for you to become? And then he answers our question with a simple, "Verily, I say unto you, *Even As I Am.*"

Contemplating becoming like him can be overwhelming and intimidating unless we remember he said it cannot be done in a day. It is even much *more* than the labor of a lifetime. And so this year I want to add something more meaningful to that original statement. If you could see the woman that God intends for you to become, you would rise up and never be the same again, *and again, and again, and again, and again, and again, and again!* For that is indeed the labor of a lifetime and more!

As we struggle to fill our lives with patience, self-control, mercy, responsibility, meekness, humility, and courage, we have to remember we do these things only as we know them or have had experience with them. His perfection is beyond our reach of understanding. The most wonderful act of mercy or the most heralded display of patience that we have known does not even approach his mercy or patience. We are only seeing ourselves and acts around us in *embryo.* They are a type and shadow of things to come!

Satan would have hold upon our hearts. His approach plays on our weaknesses. He can easily persuade many that their weaknesses are so much a part of them that they cannot be overcome. Even—he convinces us—they *need not* be overcome! The message Jesus gives us is that not only can we overcome our weaknesses, but we must be consistent in our striving to do so. He teaches us that this is possible if we follow him.

Following in his footsteps is not heading toward a geographical destination but rather a *developmental* destination. His loving and serving ministry on earth gently beckoned us toward the destination with the simple words, "Come, follow me."

But Satan is in his finest hour in his *counterfeit* to stop our following of the Master. The counterfeit becomes: follow, yes, but follow the wrong "me."

I saw a beautiful and famous actress on television describing how she had "found herself." She was living with a man, and they were not going to marry because it would detract from "her." She is going to have a baby with him when she feels another need to "fulfill herself."

In a magazine I read about a wealthy industrialist who put 4,000 people out of work when he closed his factory's doors overnight without warning. He let his wife, children, home, church, pets, and business fall into ruin to "find himself" through oil painting, to "discover himself" through his paints.

On a radio station I heard a local politician pushing alternate lifestyles. He said people need to "find themselves" in whatever form of sexual expression is suited for them.

An ad in a newspaper invited readers to come to the mountains of Southern California for an encounter camp. Come to "find yourself" sexually, socially, and emotionally; to discover how and why "you" are the only one that matters.

Title of an article in a bookstore, "Looking out for Number One."

The husband of a friend of mine who left her for another woman told my friend: "Don't *I* have the right to be happy? If I don't look out for *me*, nobody else will."

And a woman who has left the Church to join in a radical wave against the Church because it inhibits "you" from "finding yourself," said, "No one should tell you what do do!"

The abortion laws were passed, the sexual revolution embraced, Women's Lib professed, prayers taken from the classroom, homosexuality opened up, and so on—all in the name of "Do your own thing and find yourself."

Satan is indeed in his finest hour. The Lord warned us that ". . . the love of men would wax cold" and men would be ". . . lovers of their own selves."

"Finding yourself" really is a stupid concept; you'd think everyone could see the weakness of it. But they don't because it is an *excellent counterfeit.* "Finding yourself" implies right away there is something wrong with us, that there is something missing, that we are no good like we are. So the concept is a two-edged dagger. One edge of the blade is selfishness, and the other edge is negative thinking!

"Finding yourself" turns thoughts *inward,* where they are jammed, crammed, and crowded in that little space in the brain. There is absolutely no room in there to sort through them, to put them in proper perspective and order. Turning thoughts *outward,* however, leaves you the entire horizon in which to place thoughts, unscramble them, and get them in order. Turning thoughts *outward* means to stop dwelling on ourselves.

"Finding Yourself" is the exact opposite of self-esteem. *True self-esteem is a liberation from self.* It is to be free from dwelling on our own wants, needs, and inadequacies! This is accomplished as we turn our thoughts *outward.* Turning thoughts inward makes us feel *power-less.* Turning thoughts outward is to lose ourselves in others. Turning thoughts to others fosters love in our hearts for others. Love for others brings great power to ourselves because loving and serving others brings us closer to becoming like the Savior.

"If ye *find* your life, ye will *lose* it. . . ." (You lose self worth as you serve yourself.) "But if ye *lose* your life for *my* sake, ye will find it."

Only as we lose ourselves in the WORK and ATTRIBUTES of
Jesus Christ will we truly "find ourselves." The WORK is people,
and it has to be done through his ATTRIBUTES. In other words, we
see ourselves and find ourselves by being as he said, "even as I am."
We must think and act and do as the Savior would think and act and
do: a labor of a lifetime, and more. And we cannot think, and act,
and do as Jesus would unless we know him.

> And beside this, giving all diligence, add to your faith
> virtue; and to virtue knowledge;
> And to knowledge temperance; and to temperance
> patience; and to patience godliness;
> And to godliness brotherly kindness; and to brotherly
> kindness charity.
> For if these things be in you, and abound, they make
> you that ye shall neither be barren nor unfruitful *in the
> knowledge of our Lord Jesus Christ* (2 Peter 1:5-10).

Faith, virtue (courage), knowledge (study, prayer, scripture
reading), temperance (self-control), patience (for ourselves and the
Lord's timing), godliness (pure thought, standing in Holy Places even
in our minds and actions), brotherly kindness (service) and charity
(the pure love of Christ) are the attributes of Jesus that we need to be
consistent in striving to obtain; not perfected in, but consistent in our
striving to grasp them.

> Wherefore, my beloved brethren, if ye have not
> charity, ye are nothing, for *charity never faileth.*
> Wherefore, cleave unto charity, which is the greatest of
> all, for all things must fail—
> But charity is the pure love of Christ, and it endureth
> forever; and whoso is found possessed of it at the last day,
> it shall be well with him.
> Wherefore, my beloved brethren, pray unto the
> Father with all the energy of heart, that ye may be filled
> with this love, which he hath bestowed upon all who are
> true followers of his Son, Jesus Christ. . . . (Moroni
> 7:46-48).

If we don't have charity, we will feel *power-less.* Charity never faileth what? Charity never faileth *us!* It will give us POWER.

Read the Scriptures

In developing Charity and becoming even as Jesus is, we must first read the scriptures. It is a simple request which he has repeated over and over through his prophets. When is everyone going to catch the vision of it? Sisters, I testify it *does* make a difference.

When I realized that reading the scriptures every day as a family was good but was not teaching my children the habit of personal daily scripture study, I made a chart of two hundred days. Every ten to twenty-five days I colored in a reward; the olders ones wanted money, the younger ones toys. At the end of two hundred days, a big family holiday was the reward. The incentives were heightened by the rule that if one person missed one day, the whole family was penalized five days—we all lost five days and had to go back and repeat. They truly were motivated to help each other. It became a successful family venture.

I really didn't believe it would make a difference for them. I knew they wouldn't try to understand what they were reading—especially the second-grader. But I knew that developing the habit and making them familiar with their own personal scriptures was the important goal. What a surprise I received!

The first difference I noticed was their attitude toward each other. Often, they were even kind to each other! But perhaps the most dramatic difference was in the family prayers of my sixteen-year-old son. For years, when it was his turn to pray, he has said the same prayer. I could close my eyes and mouth every word in the right order as he prayed it. Despite family home evenings on more meaningful prayers and so forth, he consistently continued to pray repetitiously. I noticed a real difference after about two weeks of our scripture program. His prayers began to change. They were sounding a little like the language of the scriptures!

The Lord said to do it. Why, if it doesn't matter? It *does* matter! How can we become like him if we don't know him? We know him through his teachings in his holy words in the scriptures.

Find the Good

Second, we need to practice changing our critical attitude toward our fellowmen. We need to get in the habit of looking for something to praise. Once we start judging, it becomes a *habit* to be critical. I have seen this nearly split a family.

If you dislike someone, make a list of everything you can possibly admire about that person. Concentrate on the good qualities. Everyone has good qualities. I love Sister Camilla Kimball's personal motto, "Never withhold a generous thought." Again, I've tried it, and it works; I promise you if you try it consistently, it will change your life *again.* It is important that you be sincere. Insincerity is easily discerned, and nothing is accomplished. Being sincere means being humble at this entire task.

Forgive Others

Third, practice believing in people and trusting people. Maybe you've been stung. Maybe you have been cheated, betrayed, lied to; maybe your best was disloyal. Yes, we all get stung. But you can't let that kill your faith in people. We have to continue to make the effort to have great expectations for others. Jesus did for all of us. And oh, how he was stung!

We should pray for our enemies, pray to be able to forgive, pray and keep praying, even though we don't feel one bit better about the person. Somewhere between seven and seventy times seven, the Lord will soften our hearts, and we will be able to forgive. A sweet friend shared with me the story of how she hated a man who married her best friend. He had used and abused his wife, sexually, emotionally, and physically. He had left the Church, committed adultery and hurt his wife and children more than my friend could bear. The family moved away, and the wife didn't communicate with my friend. Years passed. One evening this family's name was mentioned, and my friend "saw red" again! She swore on her breath she hated the fellow and could never, never, never forgive him.

A few months later during a Relief Society lesson on forgiveness, she felt an overwhelming need to try to forgive this man. She read D&C 64:9-11:

Wherefore, I say unto you, that ye ought to forgive one another; for he that forgiveth not his brother his trespasses standeth condemned before the Lord; for there remaineth in him the greater sin.

I, the Lord, will forgive whom I will forgive, but of you it is required to forgive all men.

And ye ought to say in your hearts—let God judge between me and thee, and reward thee according to thy deeds.

The word *required* struck hard! She began to repent and prayed and prayed to forgive him. Several more years passed before she felt she had finally forgiven him. Then one day a letter came in the mail. It was from her long lost friend.

It was pages and pages filled with ten years of catching up, the moves, the trials, the sorrows and joys. The greatest joy had been that her wayward husband had *experienced a mighty change in his heart* and had fully repented. He had spent the past five or six years making it up to her, making her his queen on a throne. He loved her and worshiped her. And, he was the bishop of their ward!

As she read this letter, my friend realized that he had been the bishop *before* she had forgiven him. He had repented and been forgiven by the Lord *long* before she had forgiven him. Suddenly she saw clearly it had not ever been her place to forgive him, that it was the Lord's choice. Of her, it had been *required* to forgive.

We should pray for the sick, the needy, the desperate, the homeless, the fatherless, the widows, old, and orphaned. We should pray for all those who need a comforting hand; we should pray to be a comforting hand.

Serve Others

Last, but not least, we should serve our fellowmen in order to learn to love them. Do you want to be irresistible to others? Who are the most irresistible people on the face of the earth to you? Who are they? The most irresistible people to you are the ones who love you.

A woman complained to me in the gall of bitterness that she had no friends; no one loved her. I asked her to try an experiment and for thirty days serve someone different each day. She tried half-heartedly and reported back that at least it took her mind off her troubles. Now what? I said, now double it, and serve someone different for sixty days. She fumed, thinking my answer a pacifier. But she tried, this time with more effort. She soon discovered there were others out there with troubles, too. Then she reported back, and I told her to triple it and serve for ninety days. She reported back three months later that she had not only served ninety consecutive days, but she had joined Candy Stripers, too! Then *she* asked me if she could do it for one hundred twenty days!

At the end of one hundred twenty more days she was a changed woman. Nearly a year had passed since her first communication with me. When she had thoughts turned inward, she was miserable, *powerless;* but when she turned thoughts outward, toward others, she began to grow in power.

She reported that her birthday was filled with flowers and cards. She said that on one special day one morning her doorbell rang, and when she opened it, she found a bouquet of flowers and a note. "Thank you for being there when I needed someone." She told me there were always notes in her mailbox, notes of gratitude for her help. She said often cookies were left in her car or doorstep. She wept with joy as she said, "I have so many friends my heart runneth over with joy!" You see, she had become irresistible to many because she loved them first.

As love is discussed in 1 John 4, many great ideas are presented. But the one I like most is the one that explains why Jesus was so irresistible. He didn't draw crowds; he drew multitudes.

We love him, because he *first* loved us (John 4:19).

An apostle told the story of a woman who came to church with the missionaries because she was interested in the Church. She moved in on the pew and sat next to a boy of about five or six years old. The Elders sat on the other side of her. The sacrament was blessed and passed. The Elders had previously explained that the sacrament was a renewal of baptismal covenants, so when it was passed to her she didn't take any bread and passed the tray to the little boy. He took a piece and held it; then looked up at her. With genuine concern for her, carefully he broke the little morsel of bread in half and extended her the invitation to take it. Tears filled her eyes, and she said, "If this is the kind of love this Church teaches, I want to become a member," and she did. For her, the little boy had been irresistible.

This is part of a letter I received this summer.

Dear Anita:

Last fall I wrote you a letter at Education Week about my mother. . . . I told you how concerned I was because my mother's self-esteem was so low that she caused herself to go into spells of starving herself. . . . I told you of my plans to bring her home with me to live. . . . I want to share with you my experience of her in the past year since I brought her home. . . .

I drove back with her to Salt Lake City to move her things out of the apartment and store them. It was a difficult, emotional thing, especially for her to do, but we did it, and when it was over, she was very anxious to get back to California. The next three months were a little rough, but she told everyone that last Christmas with us was the best she'd had in a long time.

In January she decided to look into some volunteer work at the hospital. She had worked in Central Supply several years ago. In February we saw an ad in the paper for the Green Thumb program at our local Junior College. At first she dismissed the idea of even going back to college, but with much persuasion she attended the first meeting. Green Thumb is a government sponsored program to help aid people fifty-five years of age and older to become involved in a health home-care program. The government pays all costs to send these people for two months to take health classes at college. It also involves work experience at the local rest and convalescent homes. They even graduate!

Well, mother qualified to attend, took all the classes, and graduated. Immediately following graduation she was bombarded with calls from people who did not want to place their sick relatives in a "home"; instead wanted professional help brought to their homes. Since May she has been working, taking care of sick, elderly people, and loving it. Her whole attitude toward life has changed, and she just recently purchased her own car. She is pretty much self-sufficient and this has caused her self-esteem to blossom.

She continues to live with us, in her own room, but to a great extent leads her own life. We are so proud of her, and let her know it. And she has made some special friends there, too. . . . *At 62 I feel that she has really made some right choices to pick herself up and make the lemonade out of the lemons.* Frankly, I am very pleasantly surprised at where her life is going and that she had it in her to achieve such marvelous changes. *I understand, also, that because she has been concerned with others and serving others, she has brought the greatest blessings into her life!*

Years ago, when the fighting between the Catholics and Protestants in Ireland became horribly intense, the missionaries were taken out of the country. The bitterness and hatred between the two religious elements were so un-Christlike, many wondered why they couldn't see this evil behavior.

A few did, particularly a handful of Protestant women who felt the children were really the ones being hurt. They felt that what was being given to them as an example was so un-Christlike it might mean the ruin of Ireland. They wanted to make an effort to re-direct hatred into love.

They sent out a leaflet advertising a meeting at 8:00 p.m. on a specific night in one of the schools. Any woman, Catholic or Protestant, who believed the "battle" was wrong and wanted to promote love and peace, should be in attendance. At 7:59 no one was in the room except the few who had started the idea. At precisely 8:00 p.m. the doors flew open and several hundred women poured in!

The meeting began. The woman in charge explained her feelings and desires for more love and peace in the country. She suggested that thinking and acting like Jesus would be the goal. Then she opened the floor to anyone who wanted to speak, and she sat down. Silence loomed for a full ten minutes. Then one woman slowly rose to her feet and said, "I want to shake hands with a Catholic." A few more minutes passed and another woman rose to her feet and slowly walked towards the standing Protestant woman. She extended her hand, and they clasped hands and stood there for another few minutes. Suddenly they broke into a full embrace and wept tears of joy and love. Soon the room was filled with irresistible women, hugging and embracing, experiencing the power of love!

There is an older couple that lives in Pioche, Nevada. They could sit home and complain of aches and pains or while away their time in the much earned privilege of retirement. But where do they concentrate their efforts? Doing work for the dead in the St. George Temple, a four-hour round trip drive from their home. They are faithful in their efforts to share their love with others in a special way. All over this world are millions of elderly pining away hours in useless existence, feeling a loneliness and selfishness to be served, feeling *power-less*. In this Church are thousands of elderly feeling great power in giving love to those beyond the veil as they serve in the temples of the Lord.

Karma is one of those people you really know cares about you. Not because she ever says it; she *lives* it. In our community of friends and Church members and neighbors, we have made it a practice after a baby is born to take dinner into the family the day the mother returns home from the hospital. Karma was there in my home when my last child was born. She hadn't been asked this time to bring food, but she arrived anyway with a wonderful banana cream pie and words of care, "I thought you needed this, too." It wasn't the pie that was irresistible; it was Karma.

Several years later we had the choice experience of adopting a beautiful little baby girl. We hadn't told our children about the baby so as to prevent their disappointment if the adoption did not go through. But when we were sure, we told them, and what excitement there was. We rushed to buy diapers, clothes, and a blanket. Later that day when we brought the baby home, I thought my heart would burst with joy.

A few days later Karma showed up at my door with a complete dinner, including dessert! I looked puzzled and said, "Why? I didn't just have a baby. I'm not recuperating." She simply said, "I didn't bring it for the baby, I brought it for you. It's still like you just had a baby. I wanted to do this for you." What Karma was saying was, "I brought it because I love you." I love her for that. To me she is irresistible.

There is a teenage girl whose father suddenly dropped dead last summer. Her home of peace and stability was suddenly thrown into turmoil as her mother was now forced to go to work to support the family. This pretty, popular head cheerleader was in her last year of high school. Her name was one of those presented to be homecoming queen. She was looking forward to a senior year filled with fun and popularity. But a greater sense of love filled her rather than a love of self.

It was with such Christ-like love that she approached her mother and said, "Now Mom, you can't change my mind. I've already decided what to do. I can't stand it to see you work so hard all day at your job and then come home and work so hard to take care of us. I know it breaks your heart to take the little ones to the babysitter, and I know that takes money away from the family, too. Mother, I love you too much. The glamour of all my senior activities doesn't matter as much as you do. So I've decided to finish school at night at the community college so I can stay home in the day and take care of the house and the family. I always knew you and Daddy loved me; now let me show you how much I love you."

The Savior often likened our attitude change in accepting him as that of becoming, not *childish*, but *child-like* (Matthew 18:3).

We should earnestly strive for our love to become even as unconditional as a little child.

One of my husband's favorite pastimes is junking through thrift stores. Truly, what is one man's trash is another man's treasure. One afternoon he took our little girl Paige with him and set her in a basket by him as he looked through old magazines. She was just two years old. He became engrossed with his "find" and wasn't paying too much attention to her. Suddenly realizing how quiet she'd been, he turned in time to observe an act of unconditional love. There was a fragile looking man nearby who was sorting through a box of shoes, carefully doing his work and placing them on the shelves. Not only did he appear to be lame in one leg, but one side of his face was horribly disfigured. One eye, an ear, and half his nose were gone. His mouth was a twisted mass of flesh.

Paige had quietly been watching him work, and when he turned and looked at her, she extended her little arms and encouraged him to come and give her a hug. He quickly turned away, but she softly spoke to him, "I love you." Slowly he turned his face to her and tried to smile. She stretched toward him again, and he shuffled closer. He put his fingers forward and gently touched her hand, then looked helplessly at my husband as if to say, "What do I do now?" Steve simply nodded in approval. This young man leaned over to hug Paige. She put her arms around his neck and squeezed him as if he were a long lost friend. Then she kissed him, right on his scarred and twisted side. As he walked away, Steve saw him wiping away his tears.

As my husband paid for his purchases and left the store, this young man met him at the door. In his hands was an old green stuffed animal. He pushed it into Paige's hands and said, "Please, let her have this" and walked away. What he was saying is that it had been a long time since anyone loved him unconditionally. And for him, it was irresistible.

We were born to bless each other's lives, to gain charity through service, to experience the power of love in becoming like the Savior. But I think it is important to mention that there is a fine line between carrying other's burdens and blessing other's lives. The line is so fine it cannot be seen with the eye; it can only be seen with the spirit. It is up to the spirit to teach us when we have crossed it.

Carrying another's burdens is not always *blessing* that person's life. If we carry a person's burden and encourage that person to become "people dependent" instead of God-dependent, it is not a blessing to that soul. The Lord wants us to be dependent on him because only he can give a particular gift that no one on earth can do.

It is the gift of peace. "Peace I leave with you, my peace I give unto you: *not as the world giveth,* give I unto you. Let not your *heart* be troubled, neither let it be afraid (John 14:27).

Not anything or anyone in or of the world can give the peace the Savior can. We can give each other comfort, strokes, shelter, food, raiment, etc., but only the Savior can give that inner peace *required* to sustain us and help us carry our own burdens. If we fail to see the fine line, it can become a thick wall!

The power of love is experienced more and more for each of us in our efforts to become like the Savior, the God of love. God is love. Of us, his sheep, it is required to love everyone.

> More and more, whatever my tasks and activities of the moment, or my thought patterns, there stands the Savior—whether in needed remonstration or in needed inspiration. What he is presses in upon me in relentless reminder of what I should be. What he has generously given me elicits deep gratitude and deepens my trust. His impending blessings are a spur to me to intensify my discipleship.
>
> I find I can do nothing without him. Yet, alas, how often he can do so little with me. It is increasingly difficult for me to sing those hymns that pay special tribute to him without becoming misty-eyed. Whether in the temple, on a highway, or in a jet airplane, the reflections and reminders about him come in waves, like refreshing yet subduing surf. And, on occasion, of a night, "I am full of tossings to and fro unto the dawning of the day."
>
> So it is that the time has come to testify not only of Jesus' transcendent actuality, but also to his resplendent personality. Through examining and describing his matchless attributes in action, I find the conclusion is inescapable; how earnestly we are to strive to accept his generous but genuine invitation and direction to become, as he has said, "Even as I am" (Neal A. Maxwell, *Even As I Am*).

The Lord is so specific to us in his symbolism, types, and

shadows. All are exacting and with the purpose to constantly bring forward in our minds and *hearts* the great plan of salvation, the witness of his life, and the purpose of our creation and existence. Even the very names of people and places are in similitude and of special significance to us as members of his church.

The name Genesis means "beginning"; Eden means "new life"; Abraham means "Father of Nations." The great marvel is, however, in the name of our Lord and Savior himself. The name Jehovah is the Hebrew verb "to be." The first person singular to TO BE is I AM.

When the Savior answered Moses' question of what he should tell the people the Lord is called, Jesus answered, "I am that I am," meaning "I am that one who is called I am. I am Jesus, Jesus I am. I am one eternal round, from beginning to end."

As we ponder this concept it becomes even more simple and clear that this double statement of the Savior is also echoed in his message that he and the Father are one in purpose and knowledge. That he came to do the will of his father and if we know him, we know the Father.

"*I am* that *I am*."
"*I am* the Son of God."
"*I am* the Father."
"Even one in me as *I am* one in the Father."

An exacting God then *shadows* our *own* thoughts and words with the vision of what he intends for us to become. As we get to know them, we literally take on their name as we say:

"*I am* a child of God."
"*I am* Anita."

These statements take on deeper meaning as we realize:

A. Our truest full potential and personality will only be complete *in* Jesus Christ.
B. Those statements are a literal taking on the *name* of Christ.
C. Those statements should be a constant reminder we are to become *one* with the Savior.

It doesn't matter if you have felt *power-less* in the past, or even if you feel no power in love at this very moment. The only important thing is that you are headed in the right direction—toward the Master, in a developmental direction. No matter where we are, we can always rise up and never be the same *again!*

Chapter Seven

The Power in Being a Woman

HAVE YOU ever been accused of "acting just like a woman?" Isn't that the most ridiculous thing you've ever heard? Of course, we act "like a woman"! We are *women!* But that statement is meant to suggest that to act like a woman is weakness. Women are the weaker sex—or are they?

If the veil could be drawn, and we could see ourselves standing among all the great and noble spirits, we would see how great and noble we are. We would hear the Lord say to us, "These will I make my rulers." Members of the Church are the great and noble; the Lord said that his sheep, then, are all the people who are members or would join his church if they heard the gospel. In other words, the great and noble spirits.

Elder Bruce R. McConkie said:

> To carry forward his own purposes among men and nations, the Lord foreordained chosen spirit children in pre-existence and assigned them to come to earth at particular times and places so that they might aid in furthering the divine will. These pre-existence appointments simply designated individuals to perform missions which the Lord in his wisdom knew they had the talents and capacities to do (Bruce R. McConkie, *Mormon Doctrine*, p. 101).

Some were called to stand as spiritual leaders; others were called to be great government leaders (like our founding fathers). Others were called to be courageous explorers (like Columbus); others were called to influence in their homes, wards, and communities. Elder McConkie continues,

> . . . Alma taught the great truth that *every person that holds the Melchizedek Priesthood* was foreordained to receive that high and holy order in the pre-existent councils of eternity. "This is the manner after which they were ordained—they were prepared from the foundation of the world according to the foreknowledge of God, *on account of their exceeding faith and good works.*

What a thrill that is for me, as a woman, to know that these Melchizedek priesthood bearers were valiant in their righteousness. In a world that encourages men not to be valiant in a testimony that Jesus is the Christ (because that shows weakness or the need for a crutch), I am thrilled to know there are men who love and honor and revere their God!

Well, you say, "Yes, I know all of that, and I believe that about talents, and gifts, and particular times and places. But the men were given a power I can see: the priesthood. What is my power in this world? What power do I have in having been born in this day and age and in the place I find myself today? I have not given a blessing, or healed the sick, or performed an ordinance. How can I know my power as a woman?

Our power as women lies in our destiny. Our destiny is to become Queens, Priestesses, Goddesses, *Rulers with Power* for all eternity—forever, and ever and ever! But, before we can talk about that clear picture of destiny and power as a woman, we must talk about those two entities that exist as embryonic God: male and female. The great and noble spirits who are destined to become Gods are *male and female.* Why, then, is there so much suffering in the world as the two sexes seem to battle against one another, instead of working in behalf of each other?

We need to spend a minute discussing how different the male and female spirits really are. We have heard all of our lives we are "equal, but different." It took me a long time to catch on that the statement was meant to pacify everybody. Nobody ever defined what "different" meant. Things are changing in recent years, but I still see the heavy cloud that looms over the issue of "Equal Rights."

A few differences I have found to exist between men and women are certainly not always the rule, but they seem generally true. For example, my husband will spend all day—even weeks—looking for a pair of shoes that are comfortable. Even if he finds a pair of the most handsome shoes he's ever seen, he won't buy them if they're not comfortable. Many times I don't even care about the pain I have to endure, as long as the shoes match my outfit! Another difference seems to be a man's ego. If he gets lost in a city or countryside, he will insist on turning here, turning there, going left, going right, trying to sense the right way back, while you are sitting in the passenger seat saying, "Why don't you just stop at the gas station and ask directions?!" Often, if you send a man to the grocery store for bread, eggs, and milk, he will also come back with crackers, cheese, and rootbeer. Men also don't seem to need many, if any, intimate friendships. When with a friend, they discuss intimacies briefly, while women, with many friends, tell *all*! And little differences seem to go on and on and on.

But really, what is the difference? What does *equal* but *"different"* really mean?

During my sophomore year in college—at age 19—I was standing on the edge of true womanhood. I yearned and longed to be everything a woman could and should be. I wanted to be intelligent, lovely, witty, charming, progressive, feminine, aware, and capable. It was about this time I became committed to making decisions and then sticking to them.

There was a person in my life at this time with whom I had a great deal of contention. I made the mistake of revealing to him a course of action I intended to pursue. I cannot remember the decision so I don't know whether it was a good or poor choice, but that doesn't matter. What matters is that I was planning and thinking and acting.

After I revealed my plans and feelings, this person suddenly said, "That's what's wrong with you, Anita. *You are so typical.* You are going to wreck your whole life. You are headed for nothing but trouble, because *you think and you lead with your heart.* You are so typical. A typical woman!"

If we had known or used the term "male chauvinist pig" in those days, I might have shouted it to him. But we didn't. Instead I turned white, my hair stood on the back of my neck, and I screamed back to him: "Don't you dare accuse me of leading and thinking with my heart! I am intelligent, logical, rational! Don't you tell me I think and lead with my heart! You, you, you. . . !"

For years afterwards, every time that memory faded in, I faded it away—but not without wincing and feeling the anger all over again.

The turning point came for me when one day, quite alone, I suddenly realized, "Anita, YOU *ARE* SO TYPICAL. YOU THINK AND LEAD WITH YOUR HEART. And Anita, it was MEANT to be that way!"

Suddenly, I caught a glimpse of the woman God intended for me to become. I realized how special women really are. I realized the great talent, no, the great ENDOWMENT, he has given us as women to think and lead with the heart. It is not a taking away from our intelligence, or logic, or reason. On the contrary, it is an addition to it! It is softness and refinement in a most brutal world.

My husband and I have observed something about each other. We've noted that if an idea or concept is presented to him, especially one that has to do with male response, and it sounds logical, or reasonable, he can readily agree with it. "Oh, sure, I can accept that." But if an idea is presented to me, especially one about female response, and I've never FELT it, no matter how logical or reasonable, there is no way I can be moved or convinced.

Do not misunderstand. I am not saying men are without compassion or women without logic. Not at all! I am saying that women have been given an extra level of sensitivity, a gate to a sanctuary, a place for reason to be refined and re-evaluated, a place to launder logic. To think and lead with the heart is an endowment from God to lace logic with feeling.

A friend of mine wanted me to join an organization with liberal views of a controversial moral subject. I declined, and she questioned whether I had been truly informed. I told her I had not but was willing to listen to her platform. For thirty minutes she presented to me the most articulate, intelligent, and logical reasoning for accepting an Anti-Christ idea. I was impressed and could have agreed, except for one thing—my *heart* told me it was wrong.

It's been labeled everything from "Woman's Intuition" to "Woman's Sixth Sense." The world has both criticized and counted on it. Call it what you want, you cannot ignore it. It is an *endowment*: a gift from God to his lovely and adorable daughters, a gift from a Father who is counting on those daughters to think and lead with their hearts, to refine and soften heavy—even evil—logic and reason.

It is my opinion that our minds and abilities are indeed equal, but that the *heart* is indeed different, and for a very explicit purpose.

What are the different but equal roles?

1. *Man's nature* is an innate desire to care for and protect women.
   Woman's nature is an innate desire to serve and to "feel after" needs of others.
2. *Man's physical role* is to provide and protect.
   Woman's physical role is to care and support.
3. *Man's spiritual role* is to be a guide, a conductor, to *lead* by the hand.
   Woman's spiritual role is to be sensitive, add refinement, to be a guiding light, *to lead by the heart.*

Again, I am not saying women are more wonderful than men, that we have all the compassion, and they have all the logic. No, I am saying we are as a second witness to each other. We need each other. We complete the "partnership" each with our equal, but unique gifts and different roles.

The traditional view of women serving men as "helpmeets" is now becoming one of utter repugnance to women everywhere. That thought "helpmeet" makes it appear as if their lives and work are more important than ours and that they have *all the power*, and we have none.

Out of this idea—"women are born to serve men"—have grown the seeds of discontent and inequality until the present day movement and term "Women's Liberation."

Those very words seem so fair because what human being wants to be a slave confined to servitude, a "helpmeet"? Our work as women seems infinitely more important and complex. The very soul of life depends on women. Aren't we the ones who need help?

· Yes, we are. Women *help meet* men's needs, and men *help meet* women's needs. We help each other with our different needs and in our different roles. We do not have to take *similar* roles. Women do not have to become like men. That is today's counterfeit.

If as women, we have been endowed with a great gift, the *strength to lead and think with the heart,* we can help our brothers meet their responsibilities because they *need* that element to soften their lives. They help us in other areas.

A new definition of Women's Liberation might reveal the idea that:

> (1) Women generally don't need *feeling* help to meet their duties. They often don't need help to feel after the spirit and take spiritual responsibilities. Women *innately feel* these things; men often have to be taught them. But because our emotions tend to make us over-zealous, men bring their gift to women in keeping zealousness in check. It is a counterbalance, a true, a perfect partnership.

> (2) To be fully liberated, a woman should be able to understand her role as "heart" in the partnership and that her greatest challenge lies not in shirking or shunning that role but rather embracing it. Only through it can we exercise the great gift we've been given, thus developing it even further, gaining more strength, more power in ourselves, gaining more power to true Godhood—man and woman together.

God, *male and female,* invited each of us, as male and female, to enter into a relationship with them. We are to love one another and love them; to bring together two whole separate entities to become one God. A man ". . . is the image and glory of God, but the woman is the glory of the man" (1 Corinthians 11:7). Just as God can have no glory and his work cannot be accomplished without righteous priesthood bearers who will—by righteous use of their power—bring to pass that work and glory, *neither can a man have any glory without the special gifts and endowment of the woman. Without her he can have no glory.* ". . . neither was the man created for the woman, but the woman for the man. *For this cause ought the woman to have power on her head.* . . (1 Corinthians 11:9-10; emphasis added).

The power of being a woman is not only divine and unique, it is as real a power as the priesthood, a steam engine, or an electrical current. We are equal, but definitely different, with a definite responsibility: *to lead with the heart.*

Liberation comes also in realizing that unless we as women exert ourselves to the fullest potential of our spirit and personality, we are of no value in this role. In other words, a woman who subjects herself to a position of weakness or groveling servitude or inequality in a relationship, cannot help the men in her life meet their spiritual responsibilities. All they can do is take care of physical needs. And that without spiritual strength *is* slavery.

Or if women—as many today are doing—try to counterfeit their true strength of feeling by assuming purely male roles, they grieve the endowment. For example, many older career women who have never had marriage or children, are wondering now if they haven't missed out on something. Having missed out on some of their opportunities to serve in womanly roles or in a working marriage partnership, are they truly liberated or truly free?

On the other hand, women who allow a man to exercise unrighteous dominion or keep her in a secondary posture of servitude are also destined for spiritual poverty. If either partner lets the other one call all the shots and be the conductor, then development and growth are unequal, and neither one become all he should be.

In this stretch for responsibility as a woman of power and strength, how can we assure ourselves from day to day that we will act very much like a woman? How can we assure ourselves of using our power as women to the fullest potential? How can we secure a powerful influence over the whole world?

Be Valiant in Your Testimony of Jesus Christ

Maria Millis was not afraid to talk of Jesus and so she helped change the world with her testimony of Christ and his principles. Maria loved Jesus. She was a kitchen maid in a home of nobility and befriended a little boy in the mansion where she labored. His name was Anthony Ashley Cooper, but history knows him as the Earl of Shaftsbury. He inherited the title from his father, who gave him everything—except love. His mother, a social butterfly, also ignored the needs of her little boy.

Each night Maria would bring the child a plate of cookies and a glass of milk. While he enjoyed these simple refreshments, she would tell him of God's great love and of the sacrifice of Jesus, and she would encourage him to kneel and pray before going to bed. Maria became a second mother to young Anthony. He would confide in her concerning his problems, and she would then counsel and soothe him—something his own parents would not do.

Young Anthony might have grown up to be like his father—a nasty man, a heavy drinker with little interest in family affairs. But instead, thanks to Maria's tutoring and love, he became a godly young man, sickened at the wretched social conditions of England's poor in the early nineteenth century. She acquainted him with oppression, with poverty, and with slum conditions; and she informed him that many children were forced to work fourteen hours a day in mines and mills with no opportunity for schooling.

Young Lord Ashley never departed from Maria's influence. He became a member of Parliament, and for years he championed the cause of working people. Because he was wealthy, he was able to give all his time to promoting reform. Determined to remove the blight of England's slums, he championed housing projects, and, despite the bitter antagonism of the profiteers, he abolished the employment of women and children in mines and sponsored an act that prohibited small boys from working as chimney sweeps.

What gave Lord Ashley the courage to persist in his reform efforts? He said it was the memory of Maria Millis' devotion to him as a boy. From his servant lady he had learned justice based on the love of Jesus.

During his lifelong crusades for social improvement, Lord Ashley endured many social snubs. He was often shunned because of his concerns for those unable to defend their own rights. But when he died ninety-four years ago, even his archenemies walked to Westminster Abbey in tribute to his faith and devotion. Two hundred religious, social, and philanthropic organizations were officially represented at his memorial service. How different everything might have been if a Christian kitchen maid had not befriended a frightened little boy by bringing him cookies and teaching him about Jesus (Brigham Young University, *Ye Are Free to Choose*, p. 21).

Learn from the Past but Concentrate on Today

We can't change the past, but each of us can dramatically change what will happen today and in the future. Never look back. Remember the old proverb that says, "Never forget in the dark what God has told you in the light."

Earlier I spoke of a woman in her late twenties who had been a prostitute and could not seem to let go of any of the searing memories of her guilt. I had simply asked her, "What did you do today to change the past? What did you do yesterday, last week, all last year, to change the past? Surely you did something." When her saddened reply was "Nothing, I've done nothing," and when I assured her that this was right because you can do nothing—the past is over—a ray of light beamed through the dark clouds, and she began to feel a sense of "letting go" or hope. Several years have passed, and she has a new life now. Good choices are a regular part of her living and experience.

It doesn't matter *where* you have been in the past, or even where you are at this very moment. The only thing that matters is that you are going in the right direction.

It isn't *what* you have been in the past or what you are today; it is what you can become that is the only important thing.

It is while you are standing in the dark of negative thoughts, in the mud of apathy, in the weeds of past mistakes or sorrows, that you will lose sight of the vision of WHO you really are!

Don't Make A Big Deal of Every Little Challenge That Comes Along

We move from crisis to crisis in this world. I have a personal motto that is in needlepoint in my house. It reads: "This is as good as it gets!"

If you've never read the book *Hiding Place* by Carrie Ten Boom, you've missed a sweet and tender story of great strength, self-esteem, and forgiveness. She was a prisoner of a German concentration camp and suffered the depraved and inhumane treatment that took the lives of so many. As I read of her day-to-day crisis of living, her effort to get a crust of bread or clean water, or newspaper to keep warm, I marveled at her attitude. She simply refused to make a big deal of every *little* (to most of us it would have been *great*) challenge that came along. Someone once told me, "I have tough days and good days. On the tough days I learn; on the good days I live."

Decide To Be A Part of What's Going On

It is so easy to shut out others and be in our own world when we suffer. There is a woman whom I love and admire very much. She was divorced after thirty-plus years of marriage. She was hurt and confused and alone again. But she made a conscious choice to be involved, and she *decided* to be a part of life, not withdraw. She became involved with other families, sharing and caring for them. She became a surrogate grandmother to many. Everywhere she went she shared her life, her talents, her love. She was deeply loved in return.

Then one day she found another companion in whom she could love and trust. They were married, and she now had even more lives to touch. She is at every party, every school play, every family gathering, and on and on. Many of the ideas and attitudes of these grandchildren are being influenced by her. She isn't doing anything profound; she is simply *doing*. It will be generations before the magnitude of her influence is really felt, but it's definitely there.

Single women often *decide not* to be a part of what's going on. Often they impose barriers upon themselves. Though our hearts go out to them as they are unable to yet make marriage a viable part of their lives, we need to encourage them to practice their own powers in being women. Perhaps they can catch the vision that wifehood and motherhood are more attitudes than status! They are spiritual visions and attitudes. Heavenly Mother planted within each of her daughters the vision and attitudes of being a wife and mother long before any of us came here to mortality. There are so many ways to mother needing children, to aid other lonely people in companionship!

A single woman came up to me after a conference and said, "I don't know why Heavenly Father has withheld the blessings of a family from me. But I will continue to remain true and fruitful, and I believe someday in the next life I will have a husband and children."

Her words truly bothered me. The Heavenly Father I know doesn't work like that. How could he "withhold" blessings from a true and faithful person? He also doesn't "punish" us like that. He wants us to become all that we can become! Suddenly I realized: of course! Through our specific callings in mortality we can become all we were meant to become through specific experiences designed for our natures and personalities! *If being a wife and a mother is a calling, then being single is a calling, too.* I have slowly begun to realize the vast amount of work that the Lord desperately needs done *that can be done by single women!*

Certainly being single has its special problems, but being married and having children has it's special problems, too! And to sisters who are single because they are divorced, I urged them especially not to believe it is the end of the world but only a new beginning.

I know from where I speak as I have been single and divorced, and a single parent. Once someone asked me, "How did you cope with divorce?" I gave some answer to pacify the question. But the question bothered me, and I didn't know why. It made me feel so uncomfortable. After some thought, it dawned on me. I didn't like the word COPE! It implied right away that I had a problem; that I was working with a crutch or handicap; that I was hobbling along. This is a weakening thought.

A woman is not a half of a whole. A woman is a WHOLE entity. Yes, she is one-half of Godhood, but not one-half of a person. *Couple* means *one*, but it consists of two (whole) people. Life for a woman does not begin, or end, with marriage and children. A woman can and must be a productive, useful person (whole) all on her own. Otherwise one can have a husband and a lot of children and still not understand the attitude and vision of wifehood and motherhood.

That attitude in simple words is service and love. *God is love.* It is not necessary to have a husband and children to understand this and catch this vision. Yes, I know that being single at times can place a person in a lonely moment. But trust me, being married can at times place a woman in a much too crowded moment.

The utopia is neither single or married; it is being a part of what is going on in the Kingdom of God! It isn't worrying about being acceptable; it is being concerned about being useful!

Single sisters, for you the sky is the limit. You will yet be mothers, mothers of multitudes and nations. Divorced and widowed sister, what a wonderful opportunity to *make* the elastic work; to be able to say. "I'm not *coping*, I'm *working*!" What unique opportunities to become powerful women!

We are living in a day when the strong will get stronger, and the weak will grow weaker. Soon we will see the day when there will be no middle. *Decide* now which part of the line you will be on. Decide today to be a part of what's going on. It is a decision, and only you can make it.

Depend on That Endowment

Don't let your hearts fail you. Go with it!

A young woman, I'll call her Jane, at a large university entered the cafeteria, got her food, and headed for a table. As she approached one, she saw another girl seated there, her papers and books scattered all around her, head bent down, arms folded. It was obvious she didn't want to be bothered.

Jane headed for another table, but a feeling came into her heart that she should go back and sit by the girl. She ignored it and looked for another place. The feeling flowed and persisted. She decided to "go with it" and walked back over to the girl. "Excuse me, may I eat here?" The girl moved her papers aside without a word of acknowledgment, and Jane sat down. Jane fought the feeling, but then gave in to it again. She talked and talked and slowly began to draw the girl into conversation. Jane felt "prompted" to ask if she was okay, and the girl began to weep. They talked for hours. When they parted, the girl grabbed Jane's arm and said, "Until this very day I didn't think life was worth it. I didn't think I had a friend in the world. Thank you for caring and for being my friend today."

What is the power in being a woman? Shakespeare tried to describe it: "Women are the books, the arts, the academics that show, contain and nourish all the world."

Mary Carolyn Daines tried:

> Women are doormats
> And have been
> The years these mats applaud
> They keep the men from going in
> With muddy feet to God.

Victor Hugo described our endowment: "Men have sight—women have insight."

But perhaps the greatest words which record woman's divine gift are those we find in the scriptures.

King Lamoni believed the prophet Ammon spoke the word of God; he believed all his words. He prayed to God and then fell to the ground as if he were dead. He was lifeless for two days and two nights, and then the servants began to prepare the sepulchre for his burial.

The queen summoned Ammon and told him that she had heard of his great powers as prophet. She said that she didn't know if the king was dead—even though others said he was. She desired Ammon's advice and help. Ammon knew the King was under the power of God, and he said to the queen:

> He is not dead, but he sleepeth in God, and on the morrow he shall rise again; therefore bury him not . . . believest thou this?

In her *mind* the queen could not comprehend Lamoni's lifeless body; her mind could not understand how such a thing could happen. But she put aside logic and led with her power, her endowment. She *led with her heart* and replied:

I have no witness save thy word . . . nevertheless, I believe it shall be according as thou hast said. And Ammon said unto her: Blessed art thou . . . I say unto thee, woman, there has not been such great faith among all the people of the Nephites (Alma 19:9-10).

And remember the story of the stripling warriors? They had never fought a battle before; they were very young boys. But as they marched to battle they had incredible confidence that they would not be killed. Why? Because their mothers told them they would not be killed:

Now they never had fought, yet they did not fear death . . . they had been taught by their mothers, that if they did not doubt, God would deliver them.

And they rehearsed . . . the words of their mothers, saying: We do not doubt our mothers knew it (Alma 56:47).

Those women had no way of knowing in their *mind* that their sons would be spared. Indeed, logic says that to send very young boys into battle for the first time would result in heavy casualties. But those women didn't lead with their minds, they *led with their hearts*, and they felt power in what they taught.

And perhaps the greatest recorded example of the power in being a woman by leading with our hearts lies in the New Testament. It is the account of an innocent young virgin in a time and place far from us today.

The angel appeared to Mary and told her she was blessed among women. Mary couldn't comprehend all this in her *mind* and was troubled.

And when she saw him, she was troubled at his saying, and cast in her *mind* what manner of salutation this should be.

The angel proceeded to tell her great things and that she would bear the Son of God. Again, in her *mind*, she was troubled and said:

How shall this be, seeing I know not a man?
And the angel answered and said unto her, The Holy

Ghost shall come upon thee, and the power of the Highest shall overshadow thee, therefore also that holy thing which shall be born of thee shall be called the Son of God ... for with God nothing is impossible.

And sweet Mary, unable to comprehend how that was possible, (who could?) simply *led with her heart* and said, "Behold the handmaiden of the Lord" (Luke 1:28-38).

Our challenge is to be powerful women, powerful in our unique ability to think and lead with our hearts; to first *feel*, then *do*, then *learn*, then *teach*.

> Cherish your visions—cherish your ideals—cherish the music that stirs in your heart—the beauty that forms in your mind—the loveliness that drapes your purest thoughts. For out of all that will grow all delightful conditions—all heavenly environment. Of these, if you remain true to them, your world will at last be built.
>
> —James Allen

Cherish your differences! Cherish your endowment, your uniqueness! I need them in my life. Bless me with your life. Teach me. Teach my children and my posterity.

The powers discussed in this book are not drives, or ambitions, or strong desires—they are real POWERS!

We have the potential within each of us to become aware of all that we are so that we can learn and teach. We may be an influence in the human condition and an influence for all eternity. We may represent the *heart* in the cold and dreary world.

President Kimball said in 1978 at the Women's Conference: "To be a righteous woman is a glorious thing. To be a righteous woman in the winding up scenes on this earth is an especially noble calling."

Then in 1979, he prophesied concerning the women of God:

> Much of the major growth that is coming to the Church in the last days will come because many of the good women of the world will be drawn to the Church in large numbers.
>
> *This will happen to the degree that the women of the*

Church reflect righteousness and articulateness in their lives and are seen as distinct and different—in happy ways—from the women of the world. . . . Thus it will be that the female examplars of the Church will be a significant force in both the numerical and spiritual growth of the Church in the last days.

Knowing what we know, as members of the true Church of Jesus Christ, we should be the happiest women on the earth. Unless we believe these things and practice them, the world won't see us as distinct and different, in happy ways, from them. We will not be using our powers within; we will not feel power in being women. We will feel *power-less.* The war rages on; Satan is relentless in his crusade to conquer the world.

But this will never befall us as we *receive* the power within us and become fluent in the language of the spirit. As we are *consistent in striving* to be perfect, the idea of perfection will not overwhelm and discourage us. Instead, that consistency will help us appreciate our uniqueness. As we *cherish our differences,* we will make things happen and take courage in this great stretch for Godhood. Much of the battleground is in our own hearts. We can win, because that ground belongs to us!

Somewhere in our neighborhoods, our houses, mansions, hospitals, and public platforms a new wave of women is moving forward. The struggle, the whining, the searching, the juggling for power are ceasing to exist. Not out on the horizon, but within the very heart of the Church of Jesus Christ are women who are coming forward with great power. You are one of those women.

Daughters of the living God, I salute you in your especially noble calling! As President Kimball's prophecy begins to unfold, you will not only be a significant force in the world, your influence will ring throughout the eternities! I know these things. I know they are true, not because they are logical, but because I feel them in my *heart!* And that is the witness I bear to you, woman to woman, *heart to heart.*

Now go, beloved friends, and do the things which the Lord has commanded you, raised you up at this particular time and place to do.

He will give you no commandment or calling that you cannot accomplish, save he shall prepare a way for you. The way prepared is through your own power: the power in being a woman! Of that I know in my *heart* and promise you it is true even in the name of Jesus Christ, Amen.